Understanding and Supporting Adult Learners

Understanding and Supporting Adult Learners

A Guide for Colleges and Universities

Frederic Jacobs

Stephen P. Hundley

JOSSEY-BASS
A Wiley Imprint
www.josseybass.com

Published by Jossey-Bass
A Wiley Imprint
989 Market Street, San Francisco, CA 94103-1741—www.josseybass.com

Readers should be aware that Internet Web sites offered as citations and/or sources for further information may have changed or disappeared between the time this was written and when it is read.

Jossey-Bass books and products are available through most bookstores. To contact Jossey-Bass directly call our Customer Care Department within the U.S. at 800-956-7739, outside the U.S. at 317-572-3986, or fax 317-572-4002.

Jossey-Bass also publishes its books in a variety of electronic formats. Some content that appears in print may not be available in electronic books.

Library of Congress Cataloging-in-Publication Data

Jacobs, Frederic.
   Understanding and supporting adult learners : a guide for colleges and universities / Frederic Jacobs, Stephen P. Hundley.
      p. cm.
   Includes bibliographical references and index.
   ISBN 978-0-470-59254-0 (cloth)
   1. Adult learning-United States.   2. Adult college students-United States. I. Hundley, Stephen P.
II. Title.
   LC5225.L42J33 2010
   378.1'9824—dc22
                                                     2010009695

Printed in the United States of America
FIRST EDITION
HB Printing 10 9 8 7 6 5 4 3 2 1

The Jossey-Bass

Higher and Adult Education Series

CONTENTS

The Authors

Frederic Jacobs has been professor of education at American University, Washington, DC, since 1985. While at AU he has served as university dean of faculties, dean of the School of Education, director of the doctoral program in Education, and director of the University Press. Prior to AU, he served as director of the Institute for Education Management (IEM) and the Institute for the Management of Lifelong Education (MLE) at the Harvard Graduate School of Education. He also served as provost and vice president for Academic Affairs at John Jay College of Criminal Justice at the City University of New York (CUNY). Fred has consulted extensively on issues related to higher education administration, adult learning, and change management. He is coauthor of *Workforce Engagement: Strategies to Attract, Motivate, and Retain Talent* (with Stephen Hundley and Marc Drizin). He holds a Ph.D. from the University of Pennsylvania and was a postdoctoral fellow at Harvard University.

Stephen Hundley is associate professor of organizational leadership and associate dean for Academic Affairs and undergraduate programs in the Purdue School of Engineering and Technology at Indiana University-Purdue University Indianapolis (IUPUI). He regularly consults, speaks, researches, and writes on issues related to learning and development, higher education administration, and human resource management. Stephen is the coauthor of *Workforce Engagement: Strategies to Attract, Motivate, and Retain Talent* (with Frederic Jacobs and Marc Drizin) and *Employee Engagement Fundamentals* (with Marc Drizin). He holds a Ph.D. from American University, Washington, DC.

PREFACE

PURPOSE OF THE BOOK

The focus of this book is on helping colleges and universities better understand and serve adult learners. Defined as individuals who are typically over the age of twenty-five or who occupy social roles that would otherwise signal adulthood, adult learners represent a large and growing student constituency in many colleges and universities. This is significant, as more and more adults who have been out of school for many years are turning to colleges and universities to start, continue, or complete undergraduate and graduate degrees or pursue learning that will make them competitive in the workforce, fulfill a professional requirement, or enrich them intellectually.

Higher education institutions and many private organizations have responded to this demand by creating innovative degree programs, educational offerings, and specialized services aimed directly at adult learners. Other campuses have strived to meet the multigenerational challenge of educating traditionally aged and adult learners simultaneously. And even on those campuses with a largely traditionally aged and residential cohort of students and few adult learners, marketplace conditions warrant an understanding, at the very least, of who adults are, what they seek from higher education, and how institutions have responded.

There are many worthwhile books about adult learners, higher education, and, indeed, even adult learners *in* higher education. *Understanding and Supporting Adult Learners: A Guide for Colleges and Universities* is differentiated from other similar and related works in that we identify common issues, and proceed to flesh them out through engaging, dynamic profiles—often involving competing and coexisting viewpoints. Each profile, developed under a pseudonym, either reflects an actual institution that has faced an issue, or represents a composite of how multiple institutions have grappled with the same issue. Each profile examines a particular *student, faculty, institutional*, or *policy* issue, often from multiple sides or perspectives, and frequently concludes with a decision to be made concerning immediate next steps or long-term considerations, or both. Thus, through the portrait of various issues, we seek to give readers an enhanced understanding on the type and nature of support needed for and by adult learners in college and university contexts. Although no one text can sufficiently address every issue adult learners face, we feel that this book will enhance awareness of, interest in, and action toward creating and sustaining institutional climates that can best attract, retain, motivate, and educate adult learners.

ORGANIZATION OF THE CONTENTS

Understanding and Supporting Adult Learners: A Guide for Colleges and Universities is organized into six chapters. Chapter One provides a backdrop of the variety of issues related to adult learners in higher education. Chapters Two through Five each have a series of profiles organized around *student issues* (Chapter Two), *faculty issues* (Chapter Three), *institutional issues* (Chapter Four), and *policy issues* (Chapter Five). Following are some of the types of issues presented in the various profiles in Chapters Two through Five:

- Credit for prior learning versus credit for prior experience
- Overstating accomplishments in the hopes of garnering experiential learning credit
- Financial aid pressures and course-taking challenges
- Peer learning dynamics: personality clashes between adult students
- Consistency versus flexibility in handling adult student issues
- Student complaints about teaching styles
- Managing expectations and setting boundaries with adult students
- Classroom management issues and adult learners
- Scheduling and access issues for adult learners
- Outreach and partnerships to expand offerings to adults
- Decision making centering on programming for adults

- Planning programs for adult learners
- Financial pressures and cost-benefit analysis for adult programs
- Resource allocation issues
- Credit versus noncredit course offerings and their impact on the institution
- Evaluating effectiveness of programs for adults

Chapter Six presents a framework—involving action steps, characteristics, and principles of good practice—which colleges and universities can use to analyze and improve their environments for adult learners.

AUDIENCE FOR THE BOOK

Understanding and Supporting Adult Learners: A Guide for Colleges and Universities is applicable to, geared toward, and appropriate for use by faculty, administrators, and senior leaders or policymakers. In settings where adult learning issues are already an institutional priority, readers will likely find the information presented in the profiles to be a sound validation of their daily reality. For individuals and institutions newer to the adult learning journey, this book will provide useful insights into understanding and supporting a variety of issues facing adults and other stakeholders in higher education.

Faculty from all types of institutions, backgrounds, and experience in working with adult learners should find the issues discussed in the profiles illuminating, inspiring, and maybe even a bit surprising. Being able to examine adult learning issues from a variety of perspectives and viewpoints—including adult learners and institutional leaders—should equip faculty with an enhanced understanding of the dynamic, pluralistic conditions that the presence of adults in higher education affords. Faculty are encouraged to read and reflect upon the profiles individually, as a team of colleagues in a program or department, or as part of a broader faculty development activity (for example, as an institution-wide faculty learning community on adult learners). The questions for consideration and discussion at the conclusion of each profile lend themselves nicely to large- or small-group discussions.

Administrators—presidents, provosts, deans, department chairs, student affairs professionals, and others—will gain an appreciation for the truly dynamic array of issues that adult learners face. As the issues in the profiles unfold, the need for a holistic, well-coordinated institutional approach to understanding and supporting adult learners will be clear. Leadership and support from a variety of departments, units, programs, and services will be needed in order to assist faculty and students in optimizing learning. Institutional administrators should appreciate the fiscal, academic, and programmatic decisions inherent in many of the profiles, and this information can provide a useful framework against which to judge the efficacy of local institutional approaches to similar issues.

Finally, *senior leaders and policymakers*—governing bodies, advisory boards, accreditation officials, and even legislators—will benefit from reading how issues that seem to point to an isolated incident have the potential to develop into larger, systemic problems if left unchecked. Discussions of access, quality, capacity, and reputation will likely resonate with policymakers. The issues presented in the profiles should also remind these influencers that most institutions no longer educate an exclusively eighteen-to-twenty-four-year-old cohort for whom postsecondary participation is their principal activity. In doing so, we hope to encourage policymakers to be cautious of creating or applying a one-size-fits-all standard in measuring institutional effectiveness in serving students.

The authors gratefully acknowledge both American University and Indiana University–Purdue University Indianapolis for their support of this project.

UNDERSTANDING AND SUPPORTING ADULT LEARNERS

Chapter One

Understanding the Context for Adult Learners in Higher Education

This chapter sets the stage for the rest of the book by providing background and an introduction to adult learner issues in colleges and universities. The chapter is organized in the following manner:

- Current and emerging realities in American higher education
- Adult education and higher education convergence
- Faculty development and adult learners
- Strategic choices facing institutions serving adult learners
- Issues and profiles for understanding and supporting adult learners

Individuals working in institutions where serving adult learners is a fairly recent development will find the information presented in this chapter a useful context from which to delve deeper into specific adult learning issues. Individuals in settings where serving adults is not new should find the information that follows a sound verification and validation of practices already developed and well under way.

Interest in adult learners in higher education is largely the result of factors such as distance education technologies, the potential of adult learners to provide additional revenue streams for institutions, the fierce competition from the private sector and other higher education institutions, and the rising interest in inter-disciplinary programs, among others (Pappas and Jerman, 2004). Because of changing demographics, expectations, competition, and accountability, in addition to other forces from within and outside the academy, interest in adult learners has been fueled at multiple levels within colleges and universities. Sometimes such interest begins at the faculty or staff level, where grassroots advo-cacy and action for adult learners is initiated by well-intentioned individuals operating in a larger organizational environment not yet aware of or responsive to adults. In other settings, specific programs, departments, or services operate as almost a college-within-a-college specializing in adult learner needs and interests. Depending on the scale and scope of adult learner involvement on campus, there may even be institution-wide championing of and support for adult learner issues. Regardless of level of inter-est—individual, department or unit, or institutional—the need for the knowledge, skills, abilities, and perspectives required to serve adult learners by those at all levels of the institution has never been greater.

CURRENT AND EMERGING REALITIES IN AMERICAN HIGHER EDUCATION

Every year in the United States, more than 500,000 college profes-sors prepare to teach classes, and more than 15 million students enroll in higher education (Fink, 2003). In 2012, total college enrollment is projected to exceed 15.8 million, and a new genera-tion of students and their attitudes, beliefs, and behaviors will be in the forefront of this enrollment boom. As a result, faculty, stu-dent affairs practitioners, administrators, policymakers, and other stakeholders must redefine teaching and learning approaches, expand services and solutions for constituents, rethink student development approaches, and modify educational environments (Coomes and DeBard, 2004). Multiple factors, including height-ened accountability, reduced funding, increased competition, and changing demographics have transformed the academic, fis-cal, and sociocultural aspects of many higher education institu-tions. Many higher education observers proclaim that to be viable in the modern era—and sustainable for the future—today's colleges and universities must strike a balance among and between delivering sound academic programs, conducting and promoting research, and engaging with the community as social institutions and places of higher learning. Institutional leaders must also meet the contemporary challenges of running large organizations with dwindling public support and greater competition from the for-profit education sector (Alfred, 2003; Burke, 2004; Finger & Asun, 2001; Lazerson, Wagener, and Shumanis, 2000; Levine, 2001; Massey, 2003; Twigg, 2003).

Higher education institutions are searching for new ways to address student needs while responding to the demands of external entities. They are, in particular, "challenged by accountability legislation, unstable state budgets, increased need and decreased funding for developmental education, rhetoric about seamless learning from kindergarten through college, high expectations from accrediting associations and grant makers, and the pressure resulting from operating in an ever-more-global society" (Amey, 2007, p. 1). Simultaneously, greater competition recognizes that public and private nonprofit institutions are not only competing with one another, but the rapid growth of for-profit, distance learning, and online institutions has introduced new entrants into many markets that now compete for the available students, instructors, and funds (Newman, Couturier, and Sessa, 2001).

Adult learners over the age of twenty-five now constitute approximately 40 percent of postsecondary enrollments (Kasworm, 2003a; Reindl, 2002; Schroeder, 2003; Swail, 2002). The trend in adult enrollment is not new. From 1970 to 1990, adult students increased from 28 percent to 43 percent of total undergraduate enrollment (U.S. Department of Education, 2002). Over six million adult undergraduate and graduate students were enrolled in 2000, more than the total collegiate enrollment in 1968 (Kasworm, 2003b). Changes have continued over the past thirty years in the age-group percentages of enrolled collegiate students. In 1970, college students aged fourteen to twenty-one years represented over 55 percent of the collegiate population. In 2010, however, it is estimated that fourteen-to-twenty-one-year-old students will represent only about 46 percent of the collegiate population. The remaining age representation will reflect 15 percent of students aged twenty-two to twenty-four years, and over 38 percent will be adults aged twenty-five years and older (Kasworm, 2003b; U.S. Department of Education, 2002).

This demographic diversity, in part, has led King, Anderson, and Corrigan (2003) to identify several trends in student attendance patterns that are having a notable impact on colleges and universities. These include: (1) age, gender, and ethnic diversity that change student profiles; (2) attendance at multiple institutions is increasingly common and involves a number of transfers between institutions; (3) low-income students enter higher education with family obligations and goals that often vary from those of their younger and traditional counterparts and that make persistence much more challenging; and (4) working more than part-time and attending college part-time negatively affect persistence, and these student choices also impede the ability of institutions to shorten the time to degree, improve graduation rates, and accommodate larger numbers of students; and (5) public policies can respond to changing student attendance patterns by funding programs, contracting with private entities to provide services, creating incentives for private action, and mandating action through law or regulations.

Clearly, institutions of higher education are dynamic, often porous, and serve an ever more diverse student constituency. Traditionally aged learners increasingly work while they study, whereas adults who attend college often do so while working. Each type of student is starting to mirror characteristics associated with the other more and more, forcing even those institutions who serve predominantly traditionally aged learners to now become more mindful of the challenges that students face in balancing their personal, academic, and work lives. Thus, given the fluctuating nature of both adult and traditionally aged learner involvement in education, it is necessary to understand the extent to which adult education and higher education converge.

ADULT EDUCATION AND HIGHER EDUCATION CONVERGENCE

This section highlights how adult education and higher education are both enterprises and philosophical ideas that are, in many respects, converging. After first identifying and describing some of the characteristics and considerations about adult learners, information on the following topics will also be discussed: adult learner needs and expectations from higher education; program options, degree choices, and assessment methods for adult learners; educational practices that work well for all students in higher education; approaches that work well with adult learners in higher education; and, finally, adult learner motivation, retention, and success.

CHARACTERISTICS AND CONSIDERATIONS ABOUT ADULT LEARNERS

Adult learning takes place in a variety of settings, including higher education; however, adults also participate in learning that occurs decidedly outside the traditional boundaries of colleges and universities (Mcrriam and Brockett, 2007). As a result, it is useful to define who adults are, examine the extent to which they participate in higher education, and discuss the converging nature of both adult and higher education. Defining precisely who adult learners are can be challenging, as how "adult" is defined is highly contextualized (Merriam, Caffarella, and Baumgartner, 2006). Kasworm (2003a) notes that adult learners can be defined by their "nontraditional" status: (1) *status of age*—this recognizes that in some contexts adult may be a sixteen- or eighteen-year-old, but in others, it may refer to someone older than twenty-five; (2) *status of maturity and developmental complexity*—this is typically acquired through life responsibilities, perspectives, and financial independence; and (3) *status of responsible and often competing sets of adult roles*—this is typically reflected in work, family, community, and college student commitments. Students in higher education often are defined as "adult learners" or "nontraditional students" if they are twenty-five years of age or older and, more significantly, if they have taken on what would be considered adult roles and responsibilities, such as caring for children and other family members, working full time, or participating heavily in community activities (Kilgore and Rice, 2003).

Kasworm (2003c) paints a vivid description of the salient differences between traditionally aged and adult learners. Compared to their traditionally aged counterparts, adult learners over the age of twenty-five are more likely to be: taking a part-time course load; working full time; married or separated; caring for dependent children; a first-generation college student; and receiving employer aid (such as tuition assistance). This is consistent with Kim, Hagedorn, Williams, and Chapman's (2004) characteristics of nontraditional students, which are: (1) delays enrollment *(does not enter postsecondary education in the same calendar year that he or she finished high school)*; (2) attends part-time for at least part of the academic year; (3) works full-time *(thirty-five hours or more per week)* while enrolled; (4) is considered financially independent for purposes of determining eligibility for financial aid; (5) has dependents other than a spouse *(usually children, but sometimes others)*; (6) is a single parent *(either not married or married but separated and has dependents)*; and (7) does not have a high school diploma *(completed high school with a GED or other high school completion certificate or did not finish high school)*.

Sometimes, however, even traditionally aged college students behave in manners once thought to be highly "nontraditional." As Smith et al. (2004) observe, "the bucolic vision of students attending residential colleges has faded as more and more students commute, often attending two or three different institutions during the postsecondary experience. Many simultaneously hold full-time or part-time jobs and have family obligations—they step in and out of our institutions, combining a community college program with on-line courses and a residential experience" (p. 3).

Meanwhile, adult education, as defined by Houle (1996), "is the process by which men and women (alone, in groups, or in institutional settings) seek to improve themselves or their society by increasing their skill, knowledge, or sensitiveness; or it is any process by which individuals, groups, or institutions try to help men and women improve in these ways. The fundamental system of practice of the field, if it has one, must be discerned by probing beneath many different surface realities to identify a basic unity of process" (p. 41). Cranton (2006) summarizes adult learning as containing the following characteristics: it is often described as voluntary; usually self-directed; sometimes practical or experiential in nature; and is frequently collaborative and participatory.

Merriam and Brockett (2007) make specific distinctions between adult learning and adult education. Adult *learning* is "a cognitive process internal to the learner; it is what the learner does in a teaching-learning transaction, as opposed to what the educator does . . . learning also includes the unplanned, incidental learning that is part of everyday life" (pp. 5–6). A definition of adult *education* "usually includes some referent (1) to the adult status of students; and (2) to the notion of the activity being purposeful or planned" (p. 7); thus, they define adult education "as activities intentionally designed for the purpose of bringing about learning among those whose age, social roles, or self-perception define them as adults" (p. 8).

The U.S. Department of Education estimates that more than nine million adult learners are enrolled in some form of adult education through postsecondary institutions (Kim, Hagedorn, Williamson, and Chapman, 2004), but not all of these learners are seeking a degree or credential. Adult learners participate in education to "prepare for the GED; develop skills for cake decorating; become a nurse; learn English as a second language; discover the mysteries of the computer; complete professional continuing education requirements; and pursue associate's, bachelor's, master's, or doctoral degrees. Some even return to school because it will look good when they come up for their parole hearing" (Hadfield, 2003, p. 18).

Downsizing, global competition, and especially rapid technological changes are other reasons that have facilitated and encouraged learning throughout adulthood. Studies have documented that adult learners participate in higher education for reasons related to career advancement, work stability, financial support, and related life opportunities (Merriam, Caffarella, and Baumgartner, 2006). Ongoing education and training of adults has become a necessity in many professional areas (Caffarella, 2001), and more and more adults who have been out of school for many years have turned to higher education to complete degrees that will make them competitive in the workforce, fulfill a professional requirement, or enrich them intellectually (Pappas and Jerman, 2004). In many surveys, job-related reasons were the most frequently cited reasons for participation (Aslanian, 2001; Kasworm, 2003c).

Although individual adults have their own motives for participating in higher education, some external stakeholders have expectations that colleges and universities should be a catalyst for social change, providing opportunities for those who have been historically bypassed, remedying past inequities, confronting social and economic problems, and preparing the future labor force. Nesbit (2005) identifies the interconnectedness between adult education policies, teaching and learning, adult identity formation, and the relationships between class, gender, and race. From a sociocultural perspective, adults are increasingly called upon to become involved in strengthening their communities, promoting change, and enlivening our democracy. In community-based learning, universities partner with local organizations and nonprofits to provide experiences that promote the growth and development of both students and community residents. Such learning takes a variety of forms, and occurs in a variety of locations. It is characterized by individuals coming together to exercise control and influence over the direction, content, and purposes of their learning and emphasizes the community or social as opposed to the individual level of learning (Reed and Marienau, 2008). Whatever the motive for participating, Bash (2003) notes that many adult learners are pursuing studies when their responsibilities are already likely to be overextended, and placing themselves into an environment that they often perceive as hostile and frightening.

As a result of the dynamic reasons for adult learner involvement in education—in all its many forms—taking place within colleges and universities, it is clear that there is tremendous convergence between adult education and higher education. This has implications for how student expectations are managed and accommodated, the type of programs and instructional choices offered by institutions, the teaching and learning practices employed with and for adult learners, faculty development approaches to enhancing effectiveness, and other strategic choices that institutions must make as they serve adult learners.

ADULT LEARNER NEEDS AND EXPECTATIONS FROM HIGHER EDUCATION

Most adult undergraduates rely on personal funds to cover college costs and, given the demands of their jobs and families, they prefer higher education programs that are efficient and responsive to their needs and lifestyles (Aslanian, 2001). As a result, adults exhibit a high degree of goal orientation, seeking programs with clearly defined steps that help them realize their aspirations. They seek relevancy in their studies, having little patience for assignments or courses that they don't feel relate to their life or their goals; they are also practical, assertive, and demand respect from instructors, administrators, and peers (Bash, 2003). Adult students may not be as focused on campus life in the same way that younger, traditional-aged students typically are; thus, the importance of the campus experience outside the classroom to their development may not be as much of a priority for adults. However, adults can and do learn and develop through their engagement in formal higher education (Kilgore and Rice, 2003).

Adults bring experiences and wisdom into the classroom, and receive a learning experience that informs their own professional and personal practices. In doing so, they expect both effectiveness and efficiency in the learning environments and processes (Keeton, Sheckley, and Griggs, 2002). Kasworm (2003a) describes three components to adults as undergraduate students:

1. *The classroom as the defining collegiate context*—unlike traditionally aged students, adult learners did not identify a peer group or the campus experience as significant influences; rather, the classroom became the focal point for defining their college experience
2. *Learner views of knowledge in relationship to their adult life world*—tended to define learning in terms of either academic knowledge or real-life or applied knowledge
3. *Instructor actions and related program design elements*—meaning making was enhanced by instructors who integrate adults' prior knowledge and experiences into the course content by either interpersonal engagements or active or applied learning (such as case studies and projects)

Adult learners tend to come to college with more fully formed ideas and values, and with more life and work experience than traditionally aged students. In fact, adult learners may delay their completion of a course of study for many reasons, including stopping out to "have a baby, change jobs, close on a house, care for an ailing or dying parent, get a divorce, get married, have bypass surgery, start a business, or simply catch their breath" (Hadfield, 2003, p. 19). They succeed despite the challenges their multiple roles present. First, adult learners focus their learning on skills and knowledge that are applicable to their life circumstances. Second, adult students have a more complex knowledge base upon which to draw. Third, adult learners are involved with their families, communities, and careers, potentially providing a more direct, authentic connection from the classroom to real-life experiences. Finally, adult learners tend to make the most of class time to interact with faculty and other learners, thus enhancing the process and immediacy of learning (Bradley and Graham, 2000).

Wolf (2006) notes that adults bring the sum of their experiences to their educational endeavors, including their cultural values and traditions. Researchers from disparate countries and cultures have found that adult students have strong positive reactions to teachers who demonstrate cultural awareness. If teachers of adults can mediate and mitigate among different traditions and attitudes, they model for students the ways in which learning can transcend the barriers of "difference." Researchers argue that instructors, policymakers, and other stakeholders involved in teaching adults influence them beyond just conveying subject matter; teachers of adults often become role models for synthesizing cultural values and new knowledge (Finger and Asun, 2001; Kell, Shore, and Singh, 2004).

PROGRAM OPTIONS, DEGREE CHOICES, AND ASSESSMENT METHODS FOR ADULT LEARNERS

As adult participation in higher education increased, several colleges and universities sought to provide access to adult learners through direct marketing; through scheduling accommodations, such as evening and weekend classes; through collaborations with employers; and through a variety of innovative strategies, such as giving credit for prior learning and distance learning. To effectively provide access to adults, admissions and enrollment strategies must recognize that in order for adult students to be successful, the types of issues Rice (2003) identifies must be taken into consideration; these include "child care, elder care, commuting, financing, parking, class schedules that complement child care and after-school activities, part-time or full-time employment, orientation to the campus, and introduction to available support services" (p. 54). College and universities have responded to the demand by creating innovative degree programs aimed specifically at adults—many of whom may want to design their own educational programs and may change institutions if they believe their needs are not being met (Pappas and Jerman, 2004).

One example of institutions creating market-driven programs is the number of accelerated degree completion programs available to adult learners. Accelerated learning programs are one of the fastest-growing transformations in higher education and estimates are that 25 percent or more of all adult students will be enrolled in accelerated programs within the next ten years. (Wlodkowski and Kasworm, 2003). As noted by Wlodkowski and Kasworm (2003), "on-line learning, technologically mediated learning, accelerated learning, for-profit as well as nonprofit providers, and a burgeoning adult learner market have transformed higher education" (p. 14). Furthermore, Kasworm (2003b) notes the following conditions must be present in such programs: (1) *structure*—the supportive learning world of the program; (2) *relationships*—the quasi-family relationships with fellow student learners; (3) *student identity*—the beliefs of a specific student identity for effective learning and successful completion; and (4) *adult beliefs regarding learning*—paradoxical beliefs regarding engagement in accelerated degree program learning.

Those who criticize accelerated learning programs do so under the auspices of quality. They argue that such programs offer courses that are too compressed to produce consistent educational value. Yet, "when the four barometers of quality—accreditation, learning, student attitudes, and alumni attitudes—are considered, the initial evidence is that adults in accelerated programs do learn satisfactorily and in a manner that meets the challenge of conventional college course work" (Wlodkowski and Kasworm, 2003, p. 10).

Some accelerated programs operate from a hybrid delivery model, where a portion of instruction is delivered either synchronously or asynchronously via distance learning, and other portions of the course are facilitated in a face-to-face format (Martyn, 2003). In this approach, it is important to understand adults' learning objectives and resources when faculty and administrators choose a learning technology. In some cases, overcoming barriers to information literacy, retrieval, and technical skills will be necessary for adult learners to take advantage of the wealth of information available electronically (Burge, 2001). Faculty and administrators must keep in mind that the success of hybrid or online degree programs for adults is at least partly a reflection of the merger of technology and a focus on human interaction (Pappas and Jerman, 2004).

Ironically, as the higher education population and distribution methods have diversified, choices have narrowed in terms of available degrees, programs, majors, and even courses, thus intensifying the need to change the instructional process and reallocate faculty resources. This is occurring at a time when, paradoxically, an interdisciplinary curriculum may be well suited to the personal, academic, and professional learning objectives of adult learners (Pappas and Jerman, 2004). Institutionally provided data submitted to the U.S. Department of Education confirms the extent to which the academic interests of nontraditional students have narrowed in the past decade years. For example, using 1999–2000 data, more than 40 percent of students enrolled in two-year institutions who were twenty-five and older were enrolled in just six majors; in three of those majors (business, computer science, and health) students twenty-five and older comprised more than 50 percent of enrollments; similar trends are evident in four-year institutions (U.S. Department of Education, 2002).

Many adult-oriented degree programs offer content focused on business and professions; this has led to an increase in alternative credit-awarding approaches. Learning outcomes of formal workplace courses are often identical or similar to those achieved through study in institutions of higher education. Awarding credit for workplace learning can be an effective tool in recruiting adults to participate in higher education programs. Institutions have also enabled adult learners to earn credit for prior learning through a variety of means, such as College Level Examination Program (CLEP) tests, challenge exams, and portfolios documenting and describing prior experiential learning (Thomas, 2000). At the same time, many faculty struggle to find different ways of testing their adult learners' achievements, and this dynamic is often present with traditionally aged students, too. Achacoso and Svinicki (2004) note some innovative assessment methods that faculty have used in the collegiate environment, including authentic testing, testing with multimedia, portfolios, visual synthesis, and performance-based testing, among others.

EDUCATIONAL PRACTICES THAT WORK WELL FOR ALL STUDENTS IN HIGHER EDUCATION

Many of the most reported and adopted practices in higher education that are geared for traditionally aged learners also have utility and validity as sound teaching, learning, and developmental interventions for adults. In work initially presented in 1987 and expanded in 1991, Chickering and Gamson conclude that good practice in undergraduate education:

1. Encourages contact between students and faculty
2. Develops reciprocity and cooperation among students
3. Encourages active learning
4. Gives prompt feedback
5. Emphasizes time on task
6. Communicates high expectations
7. Respects diverse talents and ways of learning

—Chickering and Gamson, 1987, 1991

Similarly, Kuh et al. (2007) outlined the following factors related to student success in college: (1) academic achievement; (2) engagement in educationally purposeful activities; (3) satisfaction; (4) acquisition of desired knowledge, skills, and competencies; (5) persistence; and (6) attainment of educational objectives. Creating the conditions that foster student success in college has never been more important, since as many as four-fifths of high school graduates need some form of postsecondary education to be economically self-sufficient and to manage increasingly complex economic, social, political, and cultural issues.

Addressing the needs of students in the midst of such complexity requires a full understanding of today's students and what they bring to their new college experience (Laanan, 2006). Faculty and administrators need to manage expectations of both traditionally aged and adult learners about the aims, purposes, resources, and opportunities in higher education (Bradley and Graham, 2000; Miller, Bender, and Schuh, 2005). Often, such expectations are set and managed through innovative first-year experience courses, the goals of which include: knowing, understanding, thinking, and learning how to learn (Erickson, Peters, and Strommer, 2006). This is related to what Light (2001) advocates as part of the social environment that universities provide for their students; he calls for college and university environments that are stable, rich, genuinely diverse, and full of opportunity.

Powerful, engaging pedagogical practices don't end at the first year, either. Fink (2003) notes that lecturing has limited effectiveness in helping students: (1) retain information after a course is over; (2) develop an ability to transfer knowledge to novel situations; (3) develop skill in thinking or problem solving; and (4) achieve affective outcomes, such as motivation for additional learning or a change in attitude. Instead, he encourages what he terms *significant learning experiences.* Characteristics of significant learning experiences include both the *process*, engaged students and a high-energy level in the class; and the *outcomes*, meaningful and lasting change and value in life. He further notes the types of pedagogical strategies faculty can employ to accomplish significant learning include: role playing, simulation, debate, and case studies; writing to learn; small-group learning; problem-based learning; service learning; and online learning. This reinforces evidence reported by Tinto (1994), who speaks to the academic and social integration of students as vital to their retention in higher education; by Astin (1997), who signifies the college experience variable having the most significant impact on students' educational development was the frequency of student-student and student-faculty interaction; and by Astin, Keup, and Lindholm (2002), who conclude that institutions have strengthened their capacity to foster faculty-student interaction, student-student interaction, and student engagement in community service.

Another common way to infuse student integration and interaction is through the use of learning communities. As defined by Smith et al. (2004), learning communities "refer to a variety of curricular approaches that intentionally link or cluster two or more courses, often around an interdisciplinary theme or problem, and enroll a common cohort of students. They represent an intentional restructuring of students' time, credit, and learning experiences to build community, enhance learning, and foster connections among students, faculty, and disciplines" (p. 20). Learning communities also stress active engagement and reflection on the part of the learner.

Finally, Junco and Timm (2009) note that today's traditionally aged college students have never known a time when personal computers did not exist. Their K–12 schools were likely equipped with computers, and information technology has always been—to varying degrees—a part of their learning process. For both traditionally aged and adult learners, technology has also had an impact on the development and maintenance of friendships, research, writing, information retrieval and literacy skills, and shopping and lifestyle approaches. Many learners of all ages now routinely expect colleges and universities to host live Web chats, in-house social networking sites, university wikis, and shared virtual spaces. As a result, institutions of higher education need to leverage emerging technologies, including social media tools, to enhance student learning, build a sense of community, increase student engagement, and facilitate communication.

APPROACHES THAT WORK WELL WITH ADULT LEARNERS IN HIGHER EDUCATION

Educating adults differs from educating traditionally aged learners in several ways, and one of the most important differences is that adults have accumulated knowledge and experience that can enhance or hinder the learning experience. Adults bring experiences and wisdom into the classroom, and receive a learning experience that informs their own professional and personal practices (Blakely and Tomlin, 2008; Kilgore and Rice, 2003; Knowles, 1980). Adult educators have a long tradition of valuing learning from experience, and Bruffee (1993) intends the role of the teacher to be less the traditional expert in the classroom and more the peer of students.

Yorks and Kasl (2002) define collaborative inquiry as a systematic process that educators can use to help adults make meaning from their experience. By working together, adults examine their own lives, past practices, and circumstances, and share results of their reflections to deepen the understanding of every group member. In order for meaningful learning to take place, the first feature of collaborative learning is intentional design. All participants in the group must engage actively in working together toward the stated objectives (Barkley, Cross, and Major, 2004). They further report that "the evidence is strong—for a variety of reasons—that students who might be considered nontraditional college students prefer cooperative group learning and stand to benefit more from it than traditional students" (p. 21).

Transformative learning in adulthood, as discussed extensively by Mezirow (1990, 2000), helps adult learners tap into their rich and diverse life experiences as a basis for growth and lifelong learning. Transformative learning is essentially a process by which "previously uncritically assimilated assumptions, beliefs, values, and perspectives are questioned and thereby become more open, permeable, and better validated" (Cranton, 2006, p. 2). Such transformations are often linked to the developmental aspect of adulthood. According to Clark and Caffarella (2000), our approach to adult learners and the learning process is shaped by our knowledge of how adults change and develop across the life span, including changes biologically, psychologically, and socioculturally. Tennant and Pogson (2002) identify the critical connections between experience and learning, specifically how experience generates developmental change in adults. Depending on the maturation of the adult learner, the teacher-learner relationship can be characterized on a continuum from highly dependent to highly independent, with interdependence representing mutuality of goals and roles between teacher and learner. Interdependence promotes autonomy and self-direction in learners.

An integral part of adult education is helping learners discover a sense of meaning and purpose in their lives, a feeling of connection with something larger than themselves. Mentoring, self-directed learning, and dialogue can be used to promote learning as a way of strengthening the bond between learners and educators. When conflicts between adult learners and faculty arise, it is important to understand the impact of faculty and student behaviors on one another, recognizing that the teaching-learning relationship is a two-way street. Kramer (2003) argues for "intrusive" or "developmental advising," meaning that faculty members should take a proactive approach to connecting with students and encouraging student growth and success. Such advising involves "three concepts of shared responsibility: aligning institutional and student goals, helping students increase their capacity to take charge of their educational career, and showing concern for students by asking questions that help them make connections" (p. 5).

ADULT LEARNER MOTIVATION, RETENTION, AND SUCCESS

Student departure is a long-standing problem to colleges and universities. Approximately 45 percent of students enrolled in two-year colleges depart during their first year, and approximately one-quarter of students depart from a four-year college or university (Braxton, Hirschy, and McClendon, 2004). Improvements in instruction can contribute to increased student persistence and success for all learners. Specific recommendations for post-secondary education include more active learning, greater relevance of subject matter to adult students' lives, higher levels of student engagement, inclusive learning environments, use of the language of adult learners and their communities, and assessment of learner competence through performance outcomes (Flint, Zakos, and Frey, 2002; Wlodkowski, 2008).

For adult learners, barriers such as time, money, child-care responsibilities, transportation difficulties, and other considerations restrict adult participation in higher education (U.S. Department of Education, 2002). Additionally, Wlodkowski and Kasworm (2003) report that: (1) adult learners benefit from having significant prior college experience before enrolling in four-year colleges; (2) adult students with higher grades were more likely to persist; (3) financial aid strengthened adult student persistence; (4) lack of time was the dominant factor for leaving college, with conflicts between school and home and between school and work being the most frequently cited reasons; and (5) improved guidance and better advising were viewed by students as a positive influence for remaining in school.

Perna and Thomas (2008) propose a model of student success determined by four layers of context: the students' internal context, the family context, the school context, and the broader social, economic, and policy context. Their model makes several assumptions about student success, including: (1) student success is a longitudinal process; (2) multiple theoretical approaches inform understanding of student success; (3) student success is shaped by multiple levels of context; (4) the relative contribution of different disciplinary and area perspectives to understanding student success varies; (5) multiple methodological approaches contribute to knowledge of student success; and (6) student success processes vary across groups. Increasing the success of adult learners in higher education offers promising policies and insights. These include financial assistance, especially to low-income adults; stronger student support services, including academic advising, personal counseling, tutoring, and remediation; a commitment to adult learners with a focus on meeting their needs; and faculty and instruction responsive to adult learners (Wlodkowski, 2008).

The convergence of adult education and higher education has highlighted a variety of conditions under which colleges and universities must now be responsive. These include balancing the often competing and coexisting tensions of students' personal and professional goals versus the educational goals an institution has for its learners; viewing students as both learners and customers, something that the consumerist mentality of traditionally aged and adult learners now demands; and maintaining consistency in serving learners while being attuned to the necessary and reasonable flexibility that adult learners need in courses, options, and educational practices. All of these have implications for institutional planning, evolution, and change. One area where tremendous attention must be given is, naturally, faculty development.

FACULTY DEVELOPMENT AND ADULT LEARNERS

Success in providing access and services to adult learners has made it imperative to alter the process of teaching and learning in response to new classroom constituencies and emerging knowledge about cognitive and intellectual development across the lifespan. A "cottage industry" of faculty development programs has developed to redirect and retrain faculty whose primary previous teaching experience has been with students from the traditional paradigm. Many faculty members hold more positive views of nontraditional students than they do of traditional students (Knowles, 1980; Merriam, Caffarella, and Baumgartner, 2006). Braxton (2008) notes that there is tremendous complexity in the roles that college and university faculty play in shaping the persistence and departure decisions of undergraduate students, including adult learners. Curricular structures to instructional staffing practices to faculty teaching and learning styles can all serve to facilitate inclusiveness, engagement, and efficiency or, conversely, can be unintentional barriers to student success. Faculty preparation for teaching in adult degree programs varies from institution to institution and reflects many trends in higher education, including the use of part-time and nontenure-track faculty (Pappas and Jerman, 2004).

Several theories and approaches to adult learning have emerged which provide insight and direction into structuring learning activities in higher education and elsewhere for adults. One of the earliest and most popular comparisons between children, traditionally aged postsecondary students, and adult learners is an examination of the concepts of pedagogy and andragogy (Merriam, Caffarella, and Baumgartner, 2006; Wilson and Hayes, 2009). Pedagogy, a word with Greek roots meaning "leader of the child," places learners in a decidedly dependent mode. Learners only need to learn what the teacher teaches, and the teacher's experiences are the ones that matter most. In the pedagogical context, learning experiences are organized around the logic of the subject matter content, and learning takes place in sequential, predetermined ways. Individual learners in this approach are typically motivated by external rewards and punishment, such as grades, advancement, and feedback from the teacher. Andragogy, by contrast, derives its philosophy from German roots meaning that teachers should cooperate with pupils. In the andragogical perspective, learners need to understand why they need to learn something before undertaking the learning process. This means the learners are viewed as being responsible for their own decisions and for being self-directed, and that learner experiences are acknowledged, valued, and utilized in the learning process. Unlike pedagogy, which is teacher directed, andragogy organizes learning experiences around applications to the real-life situations of learners, and learners become ready to learn those things they need to know in order to effectively cope with their real-life situations. The result is motivation for learning that is driven primarily by internal pressures or desires on the part of the individual learner (Merriam, Caffarella, and Baumgartner, 2006; Merriam and Brockett, 2007; Wilson and Hayes, 2009).

Initially, pedagogy denoted education of young people and andragogy denoted education of adults. Ultimately, though, pedagogy and andragogy came to be viewed as anchors on a continuum that represents the relationship between teacher and learner. There are some circumstances in which learning can and should be pedagogical, some circumstances in which learning can and should be andragogical, and some circumstances in which learning is best accomplished by an appropriate blending of these two approaches. Beyond pedagogy and andragogy, there are other learning theories used in adult learning: behaviorism, cognitivism, humanism, and social learning theory (Merriam, Caffarella, and Baumgartner, 2006; Merriam and Brockett, 2007; Wilson and Hayes, 2009).

In behaviorism, the view of the learning process is focused on a change in the behavior of the learners. Its purpose is to produce a change in the desired actions on the part of the learner, and, as such, the teacher's role is to arrange the environment in such a way as to elicit the desired responses from learners. The use of behavioral objectives, competency-based education, and an emphasis on skill development and training, especially in corporate settings, is all derived from a behavioral perspective. All of this makes behaviorism closely associated with the pedagogical perspective. Cognitivism, by contrast, focuses on the internal mental processes of the learners, including things such as insight, information processing, memory, and perception, among others. Its purpose in education is to develop the learner's capacity and skills to earn better. The teacher's role is to structure content of the learning activities in such a way as to permit the cognitive development of the learner.

If behaviorism focuses on changes to behavior and cognitivism focuses on changes to internal mental processes, humanism focuses on the development and integration of the whole person. In the humanistic perspective, learning is viewed as a deeply personal act that is undertaken to fulfill one's potential. The goal is to equip the learner with autonomy and the ability to be self-directed, and to permit his or her holistic growth and development. The teacher becomes the ultimate facilitator in humanism; learner interests are paramount and serve as the basis for all learning activities. As such, humanism is most closely associated with andragogy.

Social learning theory treats learning as the interaction with and observation of others in a social context. Its purpose is to provide learners with examples of behaviors and to encourage their modeling of those behaviors. The teacher typically models new roles and guides the learning through practicing those new roles. Teachers and other learners then provide feedback to the learner on the extent of mastery relative to the new roles or behaviors. Social learning theory is especially useful in learning settings where socialization, mentoring, and indoctrination are critical for learner success. In all of the learning theories and approaches described here, learning is best achieved when new information is attached to existing knowledge and the benefits and uses of learning are made explicit to adults (Merriam, Caffarella, and Baumgartner, 2006; Merriam and Brockett, 2007; Wilson and Hayes, 2009).

Beyond mere understanding and appreciation for learning theories and perspectives that are associated with adults, there is also the need for faculty to translate these into concrete actions that can positively affect the adult learner-faculty member relationship. Vella (2002) identifies twelve principles for faculty in order to facilitate effective adult learning:

1. Needs assessment: participation of the learners in naming what is to be learned
2. Safety in the environment and the process
3. Sound relationships between teacher and learner and among learners
4. Sequence of content and reinforcement
5. Praxis: action with reflection or learning by doing
6. Respect for learners as decision makers
7. Ideas, feelings, and actions: cognitive, affective, and psychomotor aspects of learning

8. Immediacy of the learning
9. Clear roles and role development
10. Teamwork and use of small groups
11. Engagement of the learners in what they are learning
12. Accountability: how do they know they know?

Ross-Gordon (2003, pp. 49–50), too, provides a series of recommendations for classroom practice with adult learners:

1. Provide opportunities for adults to exercise self-direction in the identification of personal goals, selection of learning strategies, and modes of assessment
2. Recognize and foster relationships between academic learning and learning in the larger world
3. Recognize that cognitive development continues well into adulthood
4. Realize that many adults experience life-changing events immediately before or after enrolling in college
5. Design a curriculum that is inclusive with regard to students' cultural backgrounds, including those from marginalized groups
6. Recognize that the classroom typically serves as the focal point of the academic experience for adults
7. Make use of course designs and instructional activities that balance adult students' often mixed preferences for learner-centered and teacher-centered learning environments
8. Recognize that many return to college studies with trepidation about their abilities to be successful learners in the academic setting
9. Be sensitive to individual differences

As evidenced by these two lists of recommendations, adult education values inquiry, integrity, and commitment to equity in the teaching-learning process with adults. Vella (2007) argues that these same values are also central to democracy. She further challenges educators of adults to treat their learners as beings worthy of respect, recognized for the knowledge and experience they bring to the learning environment. One strategy to accomplish this is through what Vella refers to as *dialogue education*. This method emphasizes the importance of safety and belonging, and it is an approach that welcomes certainties and questions—from the perspectives of both the teacher and learner—in meaning making. Discussion is one of the best ways to nurture growth because it is premised on the idea that only through collaboration and cooperation with others can we be exposed to new points of view (Brookfield and Preskill, 2005). Dispositions necessary for discussions to occur in teaching-learning contexts include: hospitality, participation, mindfulness, humility, mutuality, deliberation, appreciation, hope, and autonomy (Brookfield and Preskill, 2005). At its best, "discussion greatly expands our horizons and exposes us to whole new worlds of thought and imagining. It improves our thinking, sharpens our awareness, increases our sensitivity, and heightens our appreciation for ambiguity and complexity" (p. 20).

Engaging adults in active learning is a predominant theme in higher education, and collaboration and self-directedness are central components to promote, encourage, and sustain lifelong learning (Maehl, 1999). To promote active learning, instructors across the disciplines and in all kinds of institutions are incorporating collaborative learning into their teaching (Barkley, Cross, and Major, 2004). Indeed, as Kuh (2008) notes, there are many specific curricular approaches and components that faculty can employ to engage students—including adult learners—more meaningfully and deeply in their collegiate studies. Kuh's delineation includes the following high-impact educational practices:

1. First year seminars and experiences
2. Learning communities
3. Common intellectual experiences
4. Writing-intensive courses
5. Collaborative assignments and projects
6. Undergraduate research
7. Diversity and global learning
8. Service- and community-based learning
9. Internships
10. Capstone courses and projects

Faculty are the lifeblood of any institution and the work they undertake in educating students is critical not only to the institution's reputation and sustainability, but also for the learner's effectiveness in knowing and being able to perform the intended learning outcomes. Adults represent a type of student with whom some faculty may lack familiarity in educating, and the theories, suggestions, and pedagogical practices outlined above are a small representation of the many interventions and approaches that faculty can employ to serve adults most effectively. Indeed, the amount of time, energy, and effort expended for faculty development for these purposes will often be in direct relationship to how the institution views its adult learner constituency. Therefore, if an institution is to be effective in developing its faculty to relate to adults, its leadership must make certain, strategic choices as to how the institution ultimately serves adult learners.

STRATEGIC CHOICES FACING INSTITUTIONS SERVING ADULT LEARNERS

Although state-assisted colleges and universities educate a growing proportion of all students, new types of institutions have also appeared. Nontraditional providers, for-profit colleges and universities, and institutions that use technology as their primary mode of instruction have emerged in many markets. In addition, many existing colleges and universities have reexamined and revised their missions in light of changing student demographics and enrollment patterns, and in response to what Smith et al. (2004) described as a "mismatch between student and faculty expectations, and the differences between what colleges think is important and what parents and employers want" (p. 7). Townsend and Dougherty (2007) ask three important questions concerning the mission foci of community colleges, in particular: (1) Is the societal mission of a community college to provide postsecondary education to students who might not otherwise obtain it, or to be responsive to the needs of local communities, including business and industry? (2) Should its dominant functional mission be to provide transfer education so that students can eventually attain a baccalaureate, or should the institution concentrate on workforce training and continuing education? (3) Given demographic shifts and pressures to be accountable and demonstrate student learning, are the traditional community college missions still relevant? Given the diverse constituents that higher education must serve, Townsend and Dougherty (2007) remind us that "it behooves college leaders to prioritize missions in order to focus institutional resources on those deemed most vital to their institution's goals and values" (p. 3).

As the need for information and workforce competency increases, so too have partnerships between higher education institutions and their local community stakeholders. These partnerships are particularly successful when each partner brings a different skill or experience to the relationship so that together they achieve—often more effectively—what thcy might be unable to accomplish separately. Positivc clements include shared mission, consolidation of redundant activities, strategic growth, expanded economic opportunity, and access to and conservation of resources. Partnerships between higher education and other stakeholders, particularly business and industry, must "look past the 'value-added' rhetoric that accompanies most calls for educational alliances and more closely examine for whom a partnership is of value, at what cost, for what benefit, and the extent to which it is sustainable" (Amey, 2007, p. 2). Despite the perceived benefits of collaboration, many partnerships fail to obtain desired results, cannot be sustained, or cease to benefit both parties. Some potential roadblocks or obstacles are the challenges of preparation and sustainability of the partnership, varying levels or wavering leadership support, inflexibility of one or more partners' policies, practices, and procedures, and negotiating the political and ethical consequences of the partnership (Amey, 2007; Cervero et al., 2001; Dotolo and Noftsinger, 2002; Hansman and Sissel, 2001; Spangler, 2002).

Growing student demand and government expectations have made it imperative that institutional leaders become prudent fiscal managers and aggressive generators of ever-changing revenue streams. As a result, current economic challenges and financial motivations permeate nearly every aspect of college and university leadership today and require ongoing calibration and prioritization of activities (Alexander and Ehrenberg, 2003; Dickeson, 1999). Higher education institutions are facing significant challenges in both their admissions approaches and financial aid interventions. There is growing pressure to increase tuition revenues as well as selectivity and diversity among students who choose to enroll. As a result, Crady and Sumner (2007) predict that some institutions will become smaller, some will close, new student markets will develop, and students who might have selected a more prestigious college in the past will select a more affordable college instead.

The adult learning market, which contributes to the broader economic development of a region by addressing needs for lifelong learning and an educated citizenry, also represents important financial streams for institutions. As Matkin (2004) notes, "over the past twenty years, the business model associated with adult degree programs, which focuses on the revenue they produce and the contribution margins they generate, has moved from the periphery of the institution to a more central position" (p. 61). Thus, adult baccalaureate students have become an important component in the enrollment planning and management strategy at many institutions of higher education. Rather than diluting quality, these students contributed in positive ways to both the fiscal and academic vitality of institutions. Matkin (2004) notes, "There are two markets for higher education: the residential or traditional degree market and the nonresidential, nontraditional market. One reason for making a distinction between these two markets is that it usually costs a great deal more to educate the residential degree student than the nonresidential, part-time student" (p. 62). Some colleges and universities recognize and foster the dynamism of this student population whereas others harbor animosity and mercurial attitudes toward adult learners (Bash, 2005).

Confronting an era marked by dwindling support and increased competition, it is incumbent on faculty, administrators, and higher education leaders at colleges and universities to broadcast who they are, what they do, and what makes them valuable. Strong institutional identity requires clearly recognizing your organizational strengths, effectively communicating how you are different in a crowded marketplace and building collaborative partnerships both internally and externally to promote greater awareness and recognition among key stakeholders (Anctil, 2008). Effective marketing of adult degree programs requires planning, market research, developing relevant program and services, and retention strategies that focus the unique needs and characteristics adult learners (Pappas and Jerman, 2004). It also requires what

Bash (2005) simply asks faculty and administrators to consider: What do I want my program to contain or deliver?

Finally, increasing student enrollments and exploding state needs in workforce and economic development have led to a call for increased responsiveness from colleges and universities (Burke, 2004). Bueschel and Venezia (2009) recognize that attention to college access has improved opportunities for students of all backgrounds to participate in higher education. In spite of this effort, many entering postsecondary students—especially in community colleges—are unprepared or underprepared for college-level work. Furthermore, Johnstone, Ewell, and Paulson (2002) and Tagg (2003) note that the mission of institutions is to produce high-quality learning, not simply to provide instruction. To accomplish this, Lapovsky and Klinger (2008) suggest establishing and maintaining a culture of evidence; assessing and improving institutional performance; conducting competitive intelligence about for-profit and other providers; and operating in an environment characterized by quality, efficiency, and accountability. In order for such approaches to work, an institution needs to put in place a program of five components: (1) learning goals; (2) measures of student performance; (3) knowledge of how to achieve learning with the particular student population; (4) knowledge of options for increasing productivity; and (5) institution-wide support (King, Anderson, and Corrigan, 2003). Thus, there is a compelling need to find benchmarks against which to compare and improve programs, while still maintaining the fast-paced competition for adult learners (Bash, 2005).

At the outset of this chapter, we noted that changing demographics, expectations, competition, and accountability are among the conditions that are forcing postsecondary institutions to rethink how—and to what extent—they serve their adult learner constituency. The approximately four thousand colleges and universities in the United States serve a vast market of learners, and the ability to be "all things to all people" becomes increasingly costly, potentially inefficient, and may lead to a dilution of effectiveness in other parts of an institution's overall mission (for example, research or civic engagement). Thus, the need to identify, clarify, and prioritize institutional actions is vital if important resource allocation decisions and investment in programs and initiatives are to occur with any reasonable degree of effectiveness. In determining the extent to which institutions are involved in the education of adults, there are, undoubtedly, many outstanding issues that must be understood in order for support for adult learners to be realized.

ISSUES AND PROFILES FOR UNDERSTANDING AND SUPPORTING ADULT LEARNERS

This chapter has presented background on adult learners, their involvement in higher education, and the ways in which institutions have responded to the needs and expectations of these learners. Although useful as a conceptual starting point, there are still several issues that confront faculty, staff, administrators, and policymakers as they attempt to understand and support adult learners. Chapters Two through Five of this volume delve deeper into such issues and profiles—developed and reported under pseudonyms or composites of real-life institutions—to bring these dynamics to life. Profiles are organized around four main strands: student issues (Chapter Two); faculty issues (Chapter Three); institutional issues (Chapter Four); and policy issues (Chapter Five).

Student issues include clarifying and ensuring that the right resources and solutions are provided to adult learners; assessing the college-equivalent prior experiential learning of adults; financing higher education for adult learners; and managing assignments, schedules, and peer relationships. The profiles relating to student issues address the following phenomena: credit for prior learning versus credit for prior experience; overstating accomplishments in the hopes of garnering experiential learning credit; financial aid pressures and course-taking challenges; and peer learning dynamics—specifically, personality clashes between adult students.

Faculty issues include recognizing differences and unique characteristics of adult learners; establishing clear boundaries and expectations with adult students; aligning teaching styles to meet adult learner needs; and holding adult learners mutually accountable for the process and outcomes of their learning.

The profiles relating to faculty issues address the following phenomena: consistency versus flexibility in handling adult student issues; student complaints about teaching styles; managing relationships with adult students; and classroom management issues and adult learners.

Institutional issues include ensuring that the institution recognizes adult learners as a key stakeholder; allocating sufficient resources for adult learner programs and services; making necessary changes to be responsive to marketplace demands for learning; and partnering with outside organizations to extend institutional reach. The profiles relating to institutional issues address the following phenomena: scheduling and access issues for adult learners; outreach and partnerships to expand offerings to adults; decision making centering on programming for adults; and planning programs for adult learners.

Policy issues include providing access while managing enrollment and other resource constraints; establishing decision-making criteria for evaluating adult learning programs; monitoring and improving efficiency and effectiveness of adult learning programs; and striking a balance between capacity, delivery method, and quality of offerings. The profiles relating to policy issues address the following phenomena: financial pressures and cost-benefit analysis for adult programs; resource allocation issues; credit versus noncredit course offerings and their impact on the institution; and evaluating effectiveness of programs for adults.

Each profile has been developed to provide reader engagement, interaction, and reflection on the content presented. As you read each profile, think about how such issues would be handled in your own institutional context. At the conclusion of each profile, there are questions for consideration and discussion, and at the end of each chapter, there are an action planning log and resources for further reading. The profiles are designed for a variety of uses. Faculty, staff, administrators, or policymakers may elect to read and reflect on the profiles individually. Programs, departments, or units where adult learners are a present and emerging reality may find the profiles a useful prompt in having group discussions about similar issues. Finally, the profiles would be well suited for institution-wide faculty and staff development aimed at highlighting the diversity of issues confronting both adult learners and the institutions in which they enroll. This book concludes with an experiential approach to creating, maintaining, and improving college and university contexts for adult learners. Chapter Six will provide principles and characteristics of good practice that can be employed to help individuals at any level— program or department; academic or service unit; or campus or institutional system—to analyze and improve their environments.

CHAPTER TWO

PROFILES OF STUDENT ISSUES RELATED TO ADULT LEARNERS

The profiles in this chapter cover a variety of *student issues* surrounding adult learners in colleges and universities.

In *Been There, Done That,* a group of students at St. Mary of the Meadows College in Los Angeles are disgruntled because they feel they are not receiving enough academic credit for their work experiences. The students are under the impression they will receive a large amount of credit for the number of years spent at a position, whereas the school maintains that they offer "prior learning credit" not "prior experience credit." This gap in definition has caused a group of students to be very upset, and Flora Hunt's job is to make a decision based on this information.

The Case of the Phony Portfolio involves Matina Edwards trying to get college credit based on her past learning experiences. However, she doesn't follow the steps and approaches that the college requires, and is attempting to get thirty-six hours of credit based on one project that she completed at work. Michael Kelly isn't sure that one event, however grand it may be, constitutes enough learning to warrant that much credit. Everyone at the school who has read the portfolio is of the same opinion. However, the project that Matina completed gained a lot of publicity, and not giving her the credit could create some unintended problems for the institution.

Allegra Straphos is a nontraditional student who is attempting to earn a degree while in her late thirties in *The Financial Aid Trap.*

In order to receive financial aid, she enrolled for two classes per semester, which is more than she can handle. Being a wife and mother, and working full-time, has made it difficult for Allegra to carry six credit hours. However, if she drops the class, she loses the financial aid that has allowed her to postpone payments until after she graduates. Thus, she is stuck—she really can't do the amount of work required for the classes, but can't afford to pay for one class out of pocket.

A Student's Dilemma, Part I: "This Has Got to Stop" showcases one side of the story of Cliff and Sean, students at Bedford University. Assigned to be partners in class, they started working on their assignments. Things went fine for a while, but soon Cliff stopped doing his portion of the work. He wouldn't edit papers, didn't set up interviews, and didn't complete the assignments he agreed to do. Sean has tried to be understanding and talk cordially with Cliff but there has been no change. Sean is very upset and stressed, and he feels a great amount of pressure to get the work done on his own in order to get good grades. He knows that the situation must be remedied but he isn't sure how to effect change in Cliff's behavior. How can he get Cliff to resume doing his portion of the work? He isn't sure what he will do but knows that it must be soon.

Cliff's point of view is the focus of *A Student's Dilemma, Part II: The Other Half of the Story.* Cliff feels that Sean is too detail oriented. As long as the job gets done Cliff is happy. His laid-back attitude about school is in direct contrast to Sean's. Sean wants to do everything as agreed upon, and expects Cliff to feel the same way. Cliff feels that as long as the assignments are done there is no problem. The problem is that Sean is doing the work and Cliff, apparently, is not. Cliff feels that he needs to tell Sean to relax and back off. He is as stressed as Sean is, because he feels he is being "baby-sat" by Sean. Cliff see himself as a competent veteran who will accomplish what he absolutely has to do, and he doesn't understand why Sean just can't relax.

PROFILE #1: BEEN THERE, DONE THAT (STUDENT ISSUES)

Flora Hunt glanced at her calendar, wincing as she contemplated the contradictions she would experience the next day. In the morning, she was scheduled to be the guest of honor at a breakfast at which she was to accept an award on behalf of the University from the Los Angeles Council of Colleges and Universities for "providing educational opportunities and access to working adults through creative, flexible programming, and responsiveness to student needs." In the afternoon, after she returned to campus, she had a meeting scheduled with a group of students who were appealing the decision of the amount of prior learning credit they had received. She agreed to the meeting after the students had written an angry letter in which they accused the university of "demeaning" them by dismissing their legitimate previous experiences. The learning assessment coordinator, who would also be present at the meeting, had written Hunt a memo saying that "all efforts to discuss this reasonably" had failed. Hunt often felt that she lived in two worlds: the world of rhetoric, promise, and hope; and the pragmatic world in which hard choices often led to hard feelings. Tomorrow would be one of those days.

BACKGROUND

Saint Mary of the Meadows College was one of the oldest private colleges in Los Angeles, and had a long tradition of serving the community; two of its oldest programs were in nursing and education, and for the first half of the twentieth century Saint Mary's was often the school of choice for the young women from the "better" Catholic families of Los Angeles. As time passed, the allure of a women's college diminished somewhat, and by 1970 enrollments had dropped to under 300, from an all-time high of 950. To remain viable, the college had to reach out to new constituencies, and to rejuvenate its traditional programs. One program, developed in 1974, was a post-baccalaureate certificate program to prepare people for careers in publishing. The program was well received, and within a decade enrolled approximately 100 students each year. Another certificate program, for one semester, in photography, enrolled approximately 50 students each semester.

In 1986, the college inaugurated its "Pathways to the Future" (PFP) program, designed to help working adults obtain bachelor's degrees. The PFP curriculum had four building blocks: traditional academic coursework; supervised internships at work, augmented by a seminar taught by a faculty member; credit received for a portfolio documenting and validating prior learning; and an independent study project. At least half of the credits for the degree had to be in traditional academic courses, and students could receive up to thirty-nine credits through the portfolio process.

Although there were other programs for "nontraditional" students in the Los Angeles area, Saint Mary's quickly became popular for its convenient location, and extensive weekend course offerings. In 1990, the college entered into an agreement with a large telecommunications company to offer courses and academic services at the company's downtown headquarters. By 1994, the PFP enrolled about 150 new students each year.

Flora Hunt became vice president for Academic Affairs in 1989, having served as a faculty member for eight years, three of them as chair of the education department. She was a strong proponent for adult learning programs, and had been responsible for developing a certificate program for day-care providers when she first came to the college. Many considered her to have been the catalyst for expanding PFP, and creating the partnership with the telecom company. One of her first initiatives as vice president was to obtain a $75,000 grant from a local foundation to strengthen the prior learning validation process; the funds were used to bring in consultants, support a summer workshop to train faculty, and enable the professional staff to visit programs at other institutions. Each summer, she attended the faculty conference evaluating the past year's assessment processes, and she made it a point to attend and make informal remarks at the quarterly open house sessions for prospective students. Elton Hollowell, director of the Pathways program, was one of her most trusted colleagues, and she often turned to him for informal advice. In fact, it was at his urging that she had agreed to meet with the five students, and to have Mariarosa Clemente, the learning assessment coordinator, present. Clemente's memo to Hunt outlining the controversy emphasized the students' rancor:

> [T]hree of the students are in the telecom organization's program and the other two work as classroom aides for LAUSD [Los Angeles Unified School District]. They were in the same orientation seminar and the same portfolio development course. The instructor says everything was going on well until the second [of

three] individual evaluation meetings when the instructor told two of the students that their credit requests were "probably excessive." Those students brought the matter up in class, and somehow the class erupted, with people saying they "expected" credit, and that the criteria were arbitrary. The other three students refused to attend the individual evaluation meetings unless the instructor gave them a precise formula which related "work time" to "credit hours." Now the situation has escalated, and the five students are bringing a petition "demanding" that we change our evaluation procedures from "a subjective and political" one to an "objective and measurable" one.

The Meeting with the Dean

The next day, Hunt met with the students and Clemente. She was cordial but brisk. "What can I do for you?" she said to the group. "This program has been in place for several years, and hundreds of people have received credit for prior learning, and have received degrees from the college. What's the problem?"

"The problem," said one of the students, a woman who worked at the telecom company, "is that we came into this program expecting that our professional experiences would be acknowledged and credited. Look at us! None of us has worked for less than fifteen years, and I've worked for twenty-four. Now we're being asked to describe this, explain that, get a letter from so-and-so, and then someone will say whether we're entitled to credit. I think we're being taken advantage of. If I were a full-time student here for two years, I'd have thirty-six credits. She"—the student pointed at Clemente—"thinks all I deserve is one credit for every year of work I've put in!" "Now Margaret," Clemente began, "we've been over this many times. Credit is not based on how long you worked; it's based on what you learned."

The other students joined in. "How do you know what we've learned? You can't compartmentalize all that happens on a job," said one student. Another student, one of the school aides, said: "My principal tells me all the time that I know more than most of the young graduates who come to teach in our school. Last year, one of *your* graduates, a brand-new teacher, told me she would have had a nervous breakdown without me to count on. Isn't that worth something?"

Hunt raised her hands to quiet the group: "I see that you are upset, and I want to help, but you all work and you know that within every organization there are rules and procedures and standards we all have to accept. You all knew about the portfolio development and evaluation process before you enrolled, didn't you?" The students nodded. One member of the group, the only man, raised his hand and spoke: "The portfolio process is good, and I actually learned a lot by going through the different exercises, but there's a lot—really a lot—of things I've done that don't fit anywhere, and the instructor said that I wouldn't get any credit for them. I'm thirty-seven years old, and my life and my job are only worth eighteen credits. Something's wrong!"

Clemente said, "May I say something, Dr. Hunt? I think I understand part of this problem. Students always end up with some experiences and activities that don't fit the credit structure we have in place. We always say that those experiences aren't wasted; they're just not used for credit. That's a problem everywhere."

"That's *part* of the problem," said one of the students who hadn't yet spoken, "but the real issue is that you sweet-talk us into this program, making it sound like our work experiences are worth something, and you promise 'lots of credit' and then when we get here and do the work, you say, 'Sorry, it's not worth that much, take more courses, give us more of your money.' I've attended three other colleges, and this is the same routine. Well, I've 'been there, done that,' and I want to be at a place where what I've done in my life is worth something."

Hunt continued to listen, but her mind wandered. This was the old debate about the distinction between "credit for prior learning" and "credit for prior experience," but explaining that wouldn't alleviate the students' frustration and anger. She knew that to resolve this problem she had to help the program administrators to make some changes. She thought she might be able to buy some time with the students to give her a chance to consider what options were available, and to obtain assistance from faculty and staff.

QUESTIONS FOR CONSIDERATION AND DISCUSSION

1. What are the differences between the concepts "credit for prior learning" and "credit for life experience"? How might the differences between these two concepts be best

explained? When, how, and why should such an explanation be communicated?

2. Based on the description of what occurred during the meeting between the students and Flora Hunt, what advice would you offer the college? What should be the "next steps" taken by Flora Hunt and her colleagues?

3. Determine whether your institution awards credit for prior learning. If so, what process is used to make the credit award? What are the strengths of this process? What are areas for potential improvement?

4. What are the concerns identified by the students in this case? What is the basis for these concerns?

5. What are the concerns in this case relevant to faculty or administrators? What is the basis for these concerns?

PROFILE #2: THE CASE OF THE PHONY PORTFOLIO (STUDENT ISSUES)

The two women sat in silence, staring at one another. The tension in the air was palpable. Finally, the older woman said, "You are entitled to your opinion, but I worked hard, these are my achievements, and you have no right to prevent me from receiving the credit I deserve." The younger woman stood up and walked toward the door. "We obviously disagree. Your experiences are certainly authentic, but you have not presented a credible request for academic credit, and the portfolio's incomplete and inadequate." After the other woman left, she shut the door, went back to her desk, and stood silently for a minute before picking up the phone and dialing a number. "Mike," she said, "this is Joanne. We need to talk about the problems with the portfolio, and the student's complaints. This is a mess, procedurally and substantively, and we need to figure out what to do."

BACKGROUND

Joanne Schwartz was a professor of political science and director of WELL (Work, Education, and Learning Laboratory) at Fenway College in Boston. She had been one of the founding members of "the Lab," which had started out as a collaborative project between the college and two of the largest banks in Boston to help bank employees obtain bachelor's degrees. The Lab offered seminars, workshops, and counseling, initially subsidized by the employers, to assist working adults in assembling "learning portfolios" so they could obtain academic credit for prior work experience and experiential learning, and thus complete their degree requirements more rapidly. In 1980, Fenway College obtained two grants to establish the program formally as part of its curriculum, and to open participation to any working adult. By 1994, when WELL's founding director Mel Kraft retired and Joanne Schwartz took over the leadership, the program had served over 1,200 students; in 1992, for example, Fenway awarded an average of twenty-seven credits to 93 participating students. The college also had developed a modest reputation for its innovative and high-quality work in portfolio development and assessment, and both Schwartz and Kraft were frequent speakers at professional meetings dealing with adult students.

The "merging" of work and learning was, in fact, an established part of Fenway's tradition and mission. Founded in the mid-nineteenth century as the Fenway Institute for Commercial Preparation, the institution had provided business training for Boston's financial and commercial employers for more than fifty years before offering bachelor's and, later, master's degrees. Like its larger and better known neighbor, Northeastern University, Fenway required its undergraduate students to participate in at least one coop learning experience. Nearly everyone on Fenway's faculty participated in the evaluation of portfolios at one time or another, and there was broad support for the program, and pride in its results.

THE PORTFOLIO PROCESS

The process of preparing a portfolio for evaluation had been developed and improved over more than twenty years, and had three major components:

Portfolio Planning Workshop
All students admitted to the WELL program are required to attend a portfolio planning workshop. At the workshop, they review material about the principles and philosophy of obtaining credit

for prior learning through the process of portfolio compilation. The workshop is very "hands on" with former students showing their portfolios and explaining how they assembled the material. Staff members responsible for the initial evaluation of material describe the criteria they use in evaluating material, and faculty members from academic departments talk about their roles and responsibilities.

Compilation, Documentation, and Self-Assessment

Students work independently to prepare portfolios. They can visit the WELL Center at any time to speak with staff evaluators, and most students bring in drafts of their work for review. Students can also obtain feedback through the student peer-review process through which students who have completed the portfolio process volunteer to assist those getting started. The Center retains copies of dozens of portfolios so students can see what is involved in the documentation process. Monthly voluntary seminars guide students through the self-assessment process.

Academic and Professional Evaluation

Evaluation is a two-step process after material is submitted. First, a staff member reviews the entire portfolio to make sure it is complete and clear. Although the staff member can return the portfolio to the student, rather than pass it on to academic departments for evaluation, they view themselves less as gatekeepers, and more as facilitators. Staff members cannot assign academic credit for portfolios, which can only be done by faculty members. Though a staff member can put a portfolio "on hold" and not send it on, referring it to an academic department is not a guarantee that credit will be awarded.

Once a portfolio is positively reviewed by a member of the Center staff, it is sent to academic departments for evaluation and assignment of credit. Departments have several options: no credit, credit for the amount requested, credit for less or more than the amount requested, or referral back to the student for supplementary credit. About 40 percent of the portfolios reviewed in academic departments are awarded less than the amount requested. Only rarely is more credit awarded. Appeals by students of decisions made by academic departments are referred to the Academic

Oversight Committee. Appeals by students of decisions made by staff can be appealed to the director of WELL.

The College had an established procedure which it expected all students to follow in preparing portfolios (see Exhibit 2.1), and it had formally adopted guidelines and standards, based on a scholarly study by Urban Whitaker, regarding the assessment of prior learning through portfolios (see Exhibit 2.2).

EXHIBIT 2.1: FENWAY COLLEGE WORK, EDUCATION, AND LEARNING
LABORATORY (WELL)

Guidelines and Format for the Portfolio Process

1. Attend a portfolio planning workshop

2. Compile a learning portfolio, provide documentation, and prepare a self-assessment

3. Obtain academic and professional evaluations (as appropriate)

EXHIBIT 2.2: STANDARDS FOR ASSESSING LEARNING

I. Credit should be awarded only for *learning*, and not for *experience*.

II. Credit should be awarded only for college-level learning.

III. Credit should be awarded only for learning that has a balance appropriate to the subject, between theory and practical application.

IV. The determination of competence levels and of credit awards must be made by appropriate subject matter and academic experts.

V. Credit should be appropriate to the academic context in which it is accepted.

Source: Urban Whitaker, *Assessing Learning: Standards, Principles and Procedures.* Philadelphia: Council on Adult and Experiential Learning, 1989.

Matina Edwards Enrolls at Fenway

Matina Edwards had graduated from an area community college more than twenty years before, majoring in communication skills. Her first job was at Bay General Hospital, a nationally respected research and patient treatment facility. Over the years, she advanced into a variety of administrative positions, finally becoming assistant director for Community Outreach seven years earlier. She was told at that time that she could not advance further without a bachelor's degree, so she started taking courses one at a time. Various things intervened, and after two years she had only completed nine credits, dropping some courses, failing to finish work in others, and just not getting around to registering for some semesters. She knew about the portfolio program at Fenway but thought the process was overwhelming. Three years ago she was offered the opportunity to become coordinator of the hospital's centennial celebration, a temporary position for about two years.

She jumped at the opportunity because she thought it would give her good experience and high visibility. The idea of using her work on the centennial as a portfolio project came from a friend, and Edwards was very excited that she could do a job she was really interested in and really make a dent in the credits she would need to complete a bachelor's degree at Fenway.

She attended the workshops and meetings and appeared to be very enthusiastic. She didn't hand in any of the suggested outlines and progress reports, and when asked about it she said that she preferred to submit all the material at once, and that she wanted to wait until all centennial activities were completed.

Questions About the Portfolio: Authentic Learning or Phony Pretense?

When it was finally submitted, without any prior review by staff, Edwards' portfolio request was for thirty-six credits distributed as follows: writing and critical thinking (6); psychology and sociology (6); public administration (organizational behavior) (9); communication (3); and education (personnel and program planning and evaluation) (12). Virtually all the work described in the portfolio was related to the centennial project, and she submitted two

large binders with reports, brochures, programs, and congratu-
latory letters, articles, and even an editorial in the *Boston Globe*
praising the event's success.

In the section of the narrative on *Evaluation of Learning*,
Edwards included two exhibits. One was a letter from Della
Mason, her supervisor, who wrote (in part): "You managed to solve
problems before I even knew about them, you handled difficult
people and situations with skill and tact, and, frankly, this spectac-
ular week of events would not have happened without you. You're
one in a million!" The other letter was from the chairman of the
board of the hospital: "Nothing this complex could have occurred
so smoothly without careful planning, creative leadership,
and boundless energy and patience. Everyone here, officers, board
members, professional and support staff, and our many friends in
the community are very much in your debt."

In the section on *Student's Self-Assessment*, she wrote a single
paragraph:

> This project speaks for itself. I was the "chief cook and bottle
> washer" for more than eighteen months. Some of the things I had
> done before, but most of them were new to me, and I certainly
> had never been involved in anything on this scale before. When
> I could, I asked for advice, and sometimes people suggested articles
> for me to read or people to talk to (Professor Kelly was very help-
> ful!). In the end, things were left up to me and I did the best I
> could. I don't know what I'd do differently if I did something like
> this in the future, because you don't ignore success like this.

The first reviewer, Michael Kelly, who taught the *Portfolio
Planning Workshop*, sent Edwards a memo saying he was "reluctant" to send the portfolio components to the academic departments without more detail about the relationship of the learning to
specific courses, about the theoretical (or generalizable) learning
which had occurred, and about her own reflections on the learning process. He urged her to come in and talk about the revisions
she should make. Edwards left an angry voice mail message for Kelly
saying that the portfolio was "complete" and that she had no inten-
tion of doing additional work. She sent a follow-up letter stating
that Kelly knew how many credits she would be requesting, and that

he had approved the breakdown of credits by departments. "You don't need a lot of paperwork and documentation to see what I've accomplished; you just have to read the paper. What I've done is a better demonstration of what I know than if I took a dozen tests."

Still concerned about the documentation presented in the portfolio, Kelly sent only one component for evaluation, the one for twelve credits on Personnel and Program Planning and Evaluation, to the Education Department. He included a note to his friend Chris Wolfe, who was that department's evaluator: "I don't know if this is phony or authentic. Part of me thinks this is a trumped up request for credit, and that she really didn't do anything educational while she worked on the project. On the other hand, her accomplishments are authentic enough, and there is ample public evidence of that. Do you think she has met our objectives, and has demonstrated her learning?" Wolfe's response was direct and to the point: "This is a request for praise, not a demonstration of learning. She *has* done a lot, but that was her job. To call this a documentation of learning is phony because there is nothing broader than her immediate activities that she can point to as the experience of learning. I don't consider this worth any credit in its present form." After receiving such a strong negative statement from Wolfe, Kelly then met with Schwartz to discuss the situation.

Schwartz was troubled. She told Kelly that she was worried that this could become a high visibility incident because Edwards was using work she had done in connection with the media-saturated centennial. She also said: "Mike, by expressing your own opinions to Chris Wolfe, you may have compromised his objectivity in dealing with this. Please have someone else provide a general assessment before we do anything else."

The second evaluator was Tisha McTaggert, a relatively new staff member with little experience in portfolio evaluation. She concurred with Kelly and Wolfe. "First of all," she wrote in her assessment, "the student has not conformed to the standards, particularly standards 1 and 3. Our major responsibility if we are to maintain quality control is to make certain that *every* student portfolio meets each of the standards. Furthermore, there are no real disciplinary boundaries in the portfolio, so an evaluator can't tell which part of the work is public administration and which part is education. If this were some kind of internship, the student might be able to get some credit, but this shows little if any understanding of what a learning portfolio represents. I find it weak and inappropriate."

CONVEYING THE "BAD NEWS"

Kelly was cautious and formal in his communication with Edwards. He wrote a letter indicating that the portfolio would not be forwarded to the academic departments she had requested. He acknowledged that "the activities described and your contributions to their success" were valid, but that there was too little documentation "of the learning process" to permit departmental evaluation. The letter ended: "I know this bad news will disappoint you, but further effort on your part, with assistance from staff members, and your further work and reflection, can probably result in a more persuasive and effective portfolio."

Edwards was furious and demanded to see Kelly. "You have no right," she said, "to stop my portfolio from being evaluated. Let the departments decide." Kelly held his ground, and said that the appeal for the staff decision was to the director, not to the departments. Edwards tried to appeal directly to the Academic Oversight Committee, without success. She also wrote to the chair of the Public Administration Department, but received no reply. Finally, she wrote to Fenway's president, who was a member of Bay State General's Board of Trustees. "I suggest you pursue your concerns," he wrote, "through the established processes of the College and the program." Finally, Edwards made an appointment to see Schwartz.

Alone in her office, Schwartz waited for Kelly to arrive. Although she did not think that Edwards should receive credit for the material as it had been presented, she felt that her encounter with Edwards, and Edwards' description of what had occurred, raised important issues, issues which needed to be addressed. She sat down at her desk and began to make some notes.

QUESTIONS FOR CONSIDERATION AND DISCUSSION

1. To what extent is Matina Edwards justified in her frustration at not having her portfolio forwarded to academic departments for review? Are her concerns legitimate?

2. How is learning different from activity accomplishment? How can learners be taught or encouraged to document learning processes, not just the activities and outcomes of jobs or tasks?
3. How might Fenway College improve its communication efforts, relative to the portfolio process, to current and prospective students? What type of issues must be addressed, by whom, and when?
4. In what ways would you suggest improving the portfolio development and review process at Fenway College? What advice would you provide to Joanne Schwartz?

PROFILE #3: THE FINANCIAL AID TRAP (STUDENT ISSUES)

Allegra Straphos paced nervously in the corridor outside Professor Tina Dwight's office. She again looked at the sign-up schedule for appointments posted on Dwight's door. Her appointment had been scheduled for 4:00 PM to 4:30 PM; when she arrived, late and breathless, at nearly 4:20, the office door was closed and the schedule had been changed in magic marker so that the 4:30 appointment had been changed to 4:00, the 5:00 appointment was changed to 4:45, and Allegra's appointment time had been circled for 5:15, and initialed "TD." This isn't the way I want to start this meeting, she thought, and I don't know how I can get Tina to understand everything that's happened, and why she has to help me get through this.

She walked down the hallway to the graduate student mailboxes, and picked up her mail. She hadn't had time to do that for several weeks so she had almost a dozen letters from campus offices. Her anxiety increased as she looked at each letter: overdue book fines, parking tickets, a notice from the library that a book she had requested on interlibrary loan would be held for her until—yesterday! The last letter was from the Computer Center; her check to register for the online training seminar was being returned because the seminar was oversubscribed and her application to attend had come in too late. More of the same, she thought, I am absolutely in over my head.

BACKGROUND

Gateway University is the largest private university in the Midwest, and one of the twenty-five most highly endowed universities in the United States. Situated in the middle of downtown St. Louis,

Gateway has been an integral part of the city for over 150 years, with a distinguished medical facility, and more than twenty graduate and professional schools. Unlike many institutions that developed programs for adult learners only in the last quarter century, Gateway has had a century-old tradition of opening its doors to people of diverse backgrounds, and at various points in their lives. For example, the Gateway School of Nursing started a program in 1942 that targeted older women to enter its RN/BS program. Gateway was also unique in its approach to adult learners; it had no School of Continuing Education, and all of its adult students enrolled in the programs and colleges based on their interests and educational goals. "We believe in educational mainstreaming," its catalogue states, "and students are encouraged to take courses even if they have not yet decided on a major, or even a degree program."

Enrollments of students over thirty years old had slowly increased, especially at the graduate level, from 25 percent of total enrollments in 1980 to just fewer than 50 percent in 2005. Nearly every program had some adults enrolled, and the provost's office estimated that more than 75 percent of the faculty regularly taught older students. A mid-1990s report from the regional accrediting association said: "Gateway University is a national model of the successful integration of students of all ages into its educational programs. The University's faculty and administrative staff are to be commended for the support they give to students, and for the ease with which adult learners can pursue their educational objectives."

A STUDENT WITH MANY RESPONSIBILITIES

Given its excellent track record and public commitment to adult learners, Gateway was the obvious choice for Allegra Straphos when she decided to enroll in a Master of Public Administration (MPA) degree program. Straphos was in her late thirties, and had worked in the St. Louis Department of Planning and Analysis for fifteen years, ever since graduating from the University of Missouri. Beginning as an administrative analyst, she received several promotions, and was now associate director for Federal Relations, a position of considerable responsibility, and authority for a staff of twenty-five. When she was named associate director, she was invited to participate in a two-week symposium at the University of Colorado, along with about a dozen of her counterparts from other states. She found the seminars exhilarating and the readings challenging, and decided that she was very motivated to pursue a master's program.

For her first two semesters of enrollment, she took one course each semester and did quite well, managing to keep up with her academic work while working full-time and continuing to be actively involved with her family responsibilities. She had two teenagers, and her husband was a moderately successful building contractor. Straphos had always been the bookkeeper for her husband's business, and though he was probably able to hire someone to work part-time, she felt a strong commitment to continue helping him. Money for her education, however, was beginning to be a problem. Gateway was expensive; her first three-credit course cost about $1,500; with tuition going up each year, a three-credit course now cost almost $1,700. The city of St. Louis was very supportive of its employees furthering their education, and permitted a good deal of flextime, but there was no tuition reimbursement program. She borrowed money from the credit union, but then had trouble paying back the loan. After three semesters, money was constantly on her mind.

She reluctantly concluded that she wouldn't be able to continue without jeopardizing the money she and her husband were putting aside for their children's college tuition. When she brought her leave of absence form to the registrar's office, the woman assisting her said: "Do you know that you can get financial aid if you sign up for six credits instead of three?" Straphos said she wasn't eligible because she and her husband made too much money. "This isn't a need-based program," the woman said. "It's a federally guaranteed loan program, and you don't have to pay it back until *after* you graduate. I think about half of all the graduate students have these loans. You just have to keep enrolling for at least six credits a semester."

The Trap

Straphos was intrigued, and went to the financial aid office. She was amazed at how smoothly the application process worked, and in two weeks she received a letter indicating that she was now "eligible" for the guaranteed loan program. She enrolled for two courses. Midway through the semester she told her husband: "I must be getting old. I just can't keep up with the work. Taking one course at a time seemed manageable, but this is a roller coaster." At semester's end, she received a B in one course, and a B− in the other, the two lowest grades she had received at Gateway. The next semester was even worse; in a required economics course she had to ask the professor for an Incomplete because she hadn't had time to finish the readings, or to write the paper. In the other course, with Tina Dwight, her adviser, she had gotten a C+, and Dwight had written her a note asking if "anything was wrong" because her work "was not really adequate for a graduate student." Allegra was devastated because she was very committed to her studies, because she admired and respected Tina, and because she knew that she had the ability to do well. It was just that there was so much to do, she thought, and there was never enough time to squeeze in everything that had to be done.

Three things happened at the beginning of her fifth semester of graduate study. She had completed twenty-one credits, half of the credits needed to graduate. Still taking two courses, Allegra felt she could be stretched no further. Then, suddenly, her mother, who lived close by, had a stroke, and was now permanently in a nursing home. Allegra's large and close-knit family rallied, but Allegra now had to visit her mother at least twice a week. Second, a group of students invited Allegra to join a study group to prepare for the comprehensive exams, now a semester away. She admired and respected the group members, and knew that it was important to be systematic about studying for the "comps," but the group was meeting on Saturday mornings. For four years, Allegra and her daughter Jennifer, now sixteen, had been active members of a mother-daughter hiking club that met every other Saturday morning. Last Christmas, Jennifer had given Allegra a letter which said, "I'm so proud of you because you're the only Mom who has never missed a hike, and I love you for the effort you make for us to be together." Finally, Allegra had applied to be one of ten students in a seminar on municipal, state, and federal relations that was being taught by a visiting professor, a retired United States senator. Straphos was humiliated when she was rejected for the seminar with a letter from the dean indicating that places had been given to students who had "demonstrated academic achievement and commitment."

She felt trapped and demoralized. She couldn't afford to take one course a semester, but she couldn't do the work in two courses. She had paid for, or had borrowed money for, twenty-eight credits, and if she dropped out now, all that money would be lost. She also felt that her work colleagues would lose respect for her if she quit, and that she would feel guilty about all the time she had taken to pursue this degree. These loans looked so good to me, but it was a trap, and I'm stuck, she thought.

The door opened, and Tina emerged. She beckoned for Allegra to come in, and they sat down in two chairs, facing one another. "Things haven't been going so well, have they," Dwight said. "Let me try to explain," Straphos began.

QUESTIONS FOR CONSIDERATION AND DISCUSSION

1. What responsibility, if any, does Gateway have to students who find themselves in circumstances similar to Allegra Straphos? If you were Tina Dwight, how would you react to Allegra upon hearing of her situation?
2. How might this situation have been avoided? What behaviors, policies, and approaches—and on whose part—would need to be changed in order to minimize the "trap" in which Allegra finds herself?
3. Determine your institution's policies and practices regarding financial aid and tuition payment requirements. In what ways do the policies and practices facilitate or impede the recruitment and retention of adult students? What suggestions for improvement would you make?
4. What are the concerns identified by the students in this case? What is the basis for these concerns?
5. What are the concerns in this case relevant to faculty or administrators? What is the basis for these concerns?

Profile #4: A Student's Dilemma, Part I: "This Has Got to Stop" (Student Issues)

The car behind him honked loudly, and Sean realized that the light had changed, but he hadn't yet started to move forward. He was preoccupied and wasn't paying attention. He noticed that his hands were gripping the steering wheel, a sure sign of tension. He didn't know what to do, and it seemed as if going to class each Wednesday was becoming more and more difficult. I'm not used to everything being so vague and confusing, he thought. At work, the rules are clear, and I know what my job is, and who's supposed to do what. Damn, I wish Cliff could get the message that something's wrong. He drove on toward the university, increasingly apprehensive at the prospect of meeting with Cliff, his "peer learning partner" in the master of management program. After he and Cliff met, they would go together to their class in human resource management. The reading for tonight, he thought glumly, was about conflict in the workplace. What about conflict in school? he thought. I really have to get this off my chest.

Background

Bedford University, its president often said, "is a breath of fresh air in the musty and decrepit Victorian mansion of higher education in New Surrey." Founded in 1965, Bedford was a relative newcomer in a state where six of the ten oldest colleges in the United States had been established. Surrounded by world famous private, well-endowed universities, and located in the state with the highest per capita expenditure for public higher education in the country, Bedford had nevertheless found a distinctive niche by developing bachelor's and master's programs for working adults.

Bedford's educational philosophy was based on three principles:

- Incorporating students' prior learning and professional experience into the courses taken, so that each course had a hands-on emphasis
- Empowering students to develop focused and relevant plans of study which incorporated substantial independent study and experiential learning

- Developing a support network through peer learning and mutual mentoring

The university expected all its students to be committed to its educational philosophy, and required prospective students to attend an intensive weekend workshop describing the university's approach to learning; at the workshop faculty members, current students, and alumni talked about what was unique, challenging, and rewarding about how learning took place. The Bedford University catalogue described its distinctive approach to learning as follows:

> Fundamentally, we believe that students must assume the primary responsibility for learning, using the faculty, the other students, and all their professional and personal relationships to achieve their objectives. By assuming individual responsibility for learning, and by becoming accountable to others involved in the learning process, each student becomes an active learner, not a passive recipient.

In 2000, Bedford had fifteen hundred students, two-thirds of them enrolled in master's programs. The largest of the graduate programs was the master of management program, with four hundred students in its two-year degree program. Students were admitted four times a year, and approximately half of them stayed together as a cohort for the program's duration; the remainder either accelerated their program, dropped out, or took a leave of absence. Overall, the degree completion rate in the management program was an impressive 85 percent.

The Entering Master of Management Cohort of 2006.2

Eighty-six students enrolled in April 2006 to begin the master of management program. At thirty-six, Sean Kelly was initially embarrassed at the prospect of starting graduate school so late, but he felt reassured when he looked around and saw that most students were in their thirties, and quite a few were older, with some in their mid-fifties. Sean had heard about Bedford from a friend at UPS where they both worked. After twelve years at UPS, seven of them in supervisory positions, he thought that a master's degree would help him advance further in the company.

At the orientation meeting, a panel of current students and alumni talked about the peer learning process, and explained that each student would be given a peer learning partner. "My grandmother got married in Russia at fifteen, to a man she'd never met," an alumna said, "and I thought of her when I got my peer learning partner. She had it easy. All she had to do was live with him, cook for him, and have his children. When I got my partner, I had to *learn* with him!" Everyone laughed, but she added, "I'm joking, but I am also dead serious when I say that your learning partner can make this fantastic, or can make it hell."

Sean felt lucky to be matched up with Cliff Schulman. They were about the same age, had common interests, and had similar professional goals of eventually moving into a managerial positions in human resource management. Cliff worked in the purchasing department of Simpson Systems Inc., a well-established engineering firm.

As was expected of all new peer learning partners, Sean and Cliff prepared an agreement detailing their mutual responsibilities, initially defining three areas: first, they would divide the reading for the courses they were taking, and each would prepare a written summary of key points; second, they would edit and critique each other's written drafts so that the final submissions could be improved; finally, they would interview one another, ask questions, request additional information, and, in general, supervise the compilation of each other's Portfolio of Prior Learning, a required submission due at the end of the first year of the master's program, and worth eight academic credits.

At first, the partnership worked well. Cliff and Sean used e-mail to send material back and forth. When Cliff didn't get a draft of a paper done until 1:00 ~AM, Sean got to his office at 6:30 the next morning to edit it, and send it back to Cliff for revisions. When Sean's wife had the flu and he had to miss several classes, Cliff taped them, dropped off the tapes, and then came back to deliver a photocopy of an article that had been assigned, but was only available in the Reserve Reading Room. Toward the end of the first semester, Cliff stopped preparing written summaries of the articles he had agreed to review. When Sean asked him about it he shrugged his shoulders and said, "It seems like busy work. Most of the articles are pretty easy to follow. If there's anything you really want me to do, let me know. Is that OK with you?" Sean decided not to pursue it further.

Problems in the Peer Learning Partnership

As the end of the semester approached, Sean was having some trouble in the course in managerial economics. The faculty member said his writing was "fuzzy" and the paper was disorganized. Frustrated, Sean gave the paper to Cliff, saying that he really needed help. He waited a week and then called Cliff. "Sorry, pal," Cliff said, "I've been swamped. I'll get to it soon." In class two days later, Cliff handed him the paper which had a note scrawled across the top "Looks pretty good to me. CS." There were no other comments. Sean was disappointed and decided to say something to Cliff. "I really needed help," he said, "and I was counting on some detailed feedback." "That kind of editing is not my thing," he replied, "so let's not make a big deal out of this. I want to be your partner, but there are some things I can't do." Sean thought he should say something, but then decided to keep silent.

Several weeks into the new semester, Cliff and Sean met for their weekly meeting. They had each been working on compiling a bibliography for a joint project in one of their new courses, Organizational Theory and Practice. Sean had worked all weekend, and had a bibliography and abstracts of more than forty items. Cliff had done no work. "We'll just have to go with what we have," he said, "and I'll do some extra work on the next project." Sean was furious that they would be submitting work jointly that he had done by himself. He tried to talk to Cliff about "responsibility," but it was clear that Cliff wasn't paying attention.

The Last Straw

The next week, Sean took a personal day off work to spend a day at Simpson Systems interviewing Cliff's colleagues; this was part of their original working agreement related to their collaboration on the portfolio project. Cliff was surprised when Sean appeared, saying that he thought they had agreed to another approach, and had not made any arrangements for Sean to meet with others. As always, he was apologetic, charming, and sounded sincere in his apologies. Sean tried his best to be good natured about the mishap, but it was obvious that he felt frustrated and tense. Cliff went into a frenzy of activity, trying to find people for Sean to interview, but the entire day turned into a disaster.

Now, a week later, Sean felt all the anger, frustration, and confusion returning as he approached the campus and his scheduled meeting with Cliff. This is a mess, he thought, and I really have to talk to Cliff. Tonight!

QUESTIONS FOR CONSIDERATION AND DISCUSSION

1. What are the central issues facing Sean Kelly? To what extent is he justified in his point of view, relative to his interactions with Cliff Schulman?
2. How did this situation unfold? What steps or actions could Sean have taken to avoid the deterioration of the relationship with Cliff?
3. In what ways could Bedford University provide greater structure and improved processes to facilitate an enhanced experience between learning partners? What specific strategies should be used, and why?
4. To what extent is it the responsibility of a faculty member to intervene when students fail to "get along" in the course of working together on interdependent projects? What are the likely actions of intervening versus ignoring the situation?

PROFILE #5: A STUDENT'S DILEMMA, PART II: THE OTHER HALF OF THE STORY (STUDENT ISSUES)

Cliff Schulman got back to his desk at 3:15 PM feeling frustrated and impatient. What had been scheduled as a thirty-minute "catch up and check in" meeting for 1:00 PM had just ended. The annual recommendation from his department about which suppliers of office equipment should be renewed on a sole source basis were due in another week, and the work was essentially done, but his supervisor was new, and this was the first time she was overseeing the process. So the meeting went on endlessly, repeating, restating, summarizing, checking "one last time." Instead of thirty minutes, the meeting lasted for over two hours, and Cliff still had to process some purchase orders today, or the equipment would not be delivered when it was needed.

Looking at his monitor, he saw the blinking light and the message, "You have 5 pieces of mail in your in-box." He sighed and thought, I wonder how many of them are from Sean. He retrieved them, and, sure enough, three were from Sean Kelly, his peer learning partner in the master of management program at Bedford University. He read each e-mail, growing more frustrated as he did so. Then he saw his message light flashing on his telephone console. He had seven messages, and two of them were from Sean. God, Cliff thought, he's not my learning partner, he's my parole officer. If I can't set him straight that I'm an adult, I'll have to shoot him or shoot myself.

THE ENTERING MASTER OF MANAGEMENT COHORT OF 2006.2

Eighty-six students enrolled in April 2006 to begin the master of management program. At forty-one, Cliff Schulman was a few years older than many of the other entering students, but was very self-confident and believed that he would succeed in graduate school in the same way he had been successful in his Army career, undergraduate study, and more recently in the well-respected engineering firm of Simpson Systems. He had joined the army at nineteen, obtained a bachelor's degree part-time at a large public university in Wisconsin during the six years he was stationed there, and was able to retire from the military with a reasonable pension when he was thirty-nine. His entire Army career had been spent working in military procurement, and he was recruited to work at Simpson System as soon as he left military service. He knew that his supervisors at Simpson liked his can-do attitude, and they had encouraged him to apply to the master's program at Bedford. He felt confident that he would be promoted once he finished the master's program.

Cliff had been pleased to be "paired" with Sean Kelly as his learning partner. Kelly was a bit younger, but they had similar professional ambitions. Kelly had worked for UPS since graduating college, and had been in supervisory positions for seven years. Cliff liked Sean's precise attention-to-detail attitude which, he thought wryly, was in contrast to his own more breezy and casual manner. The first weeks of their collaboration went well, and they realized that they had similar interests and preferences. Then, however, the workload in the course began to increase significantly, and so did Cliff's apprehension.

As was expected of all new peer learning partners, Cliff and Sean had to prepare an agreement detailing their mutual responsibilities. Sean volunteered to develop the initial draft, and he called several other student pairs to get ideas from them. He even talked to several UPS employees who were in earlier cohorts at Bedford. Sean came to Cliff's house one evening and brought his draft which emphasized three areas:

1. They would divide the reading for the courses they were taking, and each would prepare a written summary of key points.
2. They would edit and critique each other's written drafts so that the final submissions could be improved.
3. They would interview one another, ask questions, request additional information, and, in general, supervise the compilation of each other's Portfolio of Prior Learning, a required submission due at the end of the first year of the master's program, and worth eight academic credits.

Cliff was casual in his response. "Whatever you think will get the job done is fine with me. I'm sure we can work out any problems, but let's not worry about something that hasn't happened yet." Sean seemed to want to talk some more about the details of the agreement, but, after a moment, he said simply: "I'll make copies of the agreement and then a weekly schedule of when things are due. I'll also set up an e-mail reminder system so we can each get an automatic reminder three days before each assignment is due." Cliff paused and then said, "Whatever."

Problems in the Peer Learning Partnership

The differences in their personalities became more apparent as Cliff and Sean worked together. Once, Cliff didn't get a draft of a paper done until 1:00 AM. He had told Sean not to worry about editing it, but Sean went to his office at 6:30 the next morning, edited it, and returned the paper to Cliff. In class that evening, Cliff told Sean that it was his problem that he waited until the last minute to write the paper, and he didn't expect Sean to "bail him out" that way. Sean said he was very tired, but it was "OK."

A week later, Sean's wife had the flu and he had to miss several classes. Cliff wanted to tape all three classes for Sean, but he forgot to bring an empty cassette to one of the classes, so he was only able to give Sean two tapes. He also brought Sean a photocopy copy of an article that had been assigned, but was only available in the reserve reading room.

Sean sent an e-mail to Cliff thanking him for the material. He added: "I don't know what to do about the class that wasn't taped. I've already called a few people, and left two messages for the instructor. I'm going to class early tomorrow to ask more people for their notes. I got the article you copied for me. Page 16 is very blurry and I couldn't read it. But I will go and recopy the article so I have a legible copy for my files."

Cliff was annoyed. He said to his wife: "This is like dealing with my mother's spinster sister. No matter what you do, it's not good enough, and you always screw up something no matter how hard you try. He's turning out to be a pain in the butt."

As the semester progressed, Cliff stopped preparing written summaries of the articles even though he had originally agreed to do so. Sean "reminded" him that he hadn't received some of the summaries. Cliff said: "It seems like busy work. Most of the articles are pretty easy to follow. If there are some articles you really want me to summarize, let me know. Is that OK with you?" Sean didn't answer, so Cliff assumed it was not an issue.

Cliff used to joke with his colleagues at Simpson that "if you finish writing a report more than three days before it is due, you'll have to spend time updating it later." He was not a careful planner, and he often found himself juggling several tasks simultaneously, but, he often thought, the job gets done. Sean couldn't have been more different, and when he sent drafts to Cliff he wanted to know *immediately* when he could expect a response. If he didn't get an answer, the barrage of e-mails and phone calls began.

Cliff and Sean had a very tense exchange when Cliff took more than a week to read Sean's paper, and all he did was to write "looks pretty good to me" on the first page. He knew Sean was upset and he apologized, explaining that he was very busy at work. He said he would try to do better in the future. Sean looked at him for a minute, and then said that he would work on creating an online "tickler" system so Cliff could get daily reminders of what he needed to do for their collaborative work.

Soon after the new semester began, Cliff became increasingly annoyed by Sean's continuous monitoring of his behavior. In their course on organizational theory and practice, they had to prepare a bibliography of at least forty items. When they met, Cliff hadn't yet begun his research, but Sean had more than forty items in his bibliography, certainly enough for the assignment. Cliff knew that he should have done some work on his own, but he felt that it was "no big deal" because they could hand the paper in on time with the work Sean had done. He told Sean, "Let's just go with what we have, and I'll do some extra work on the next project." He braced himself for what had become Sean's weekly reprimands and lectures on "staying ahead of the assignment," "learning from mistakes," and "being responsible." Sean began: "Cliff, you have disappointed me again…" but Cliff was no longer listening. He was thinking to himself that he didn't know how much more he could take.

THE LAST STRAW

When they first prepared their agreement, Cliff volunteered to arrange for Sean to interview some of his colleagues in connection with one of their assignments. When he tried to set up those meetings for Sean, he ran into some difficulties. None of his colleagues was especially enthusiastic about being interviewed, and he couldn't find a single day when everyone on his list would be available. He told Sean that he thought it would be better if he conducted initial interviews by phone, and later conduct follow-up interviews in person if necessary. Sean didn't even want to hear why Cliff thought it was better to do phone interviews. He kept saying, "You made a commitment to arrange face-to-face interviews. It is written into our agreement. You said you would do it."

Finally, in exasperation, Cliff said, "Look Sean, forget about the agreement. This is a better way to get the information you need. Think about it. Do you want us to follow the letter of our agreement, or do you want to get the best information?" Sean stared at him, but didn't say a word. Cliff thought he had made his point. Several days later, to Cliff's amazement, Sean appeared at his office "to conduct the interviews." The entire day turned out to be a disaster.

Now, a week later, Cliff felt all the anger, frustration, and confusion returning as he approached the campus and his scheduled meeting with Sean. This is a mess, he thought, and I really have to talk to Sean. Tonight.

Questions for Consideration and Discussion

1. What are the central issues facing Cliff Schulman? To what extent is he justified in his point of view, relative to his interactions with Sean Kelley?

2. How did this situation unfold? What steps or actions could Cliff have taken to avoid the deterioration of the relationship with Sean?

3. In what ways could Bedford University provide greater structure and improved processes to facilitate an enhanced experience between learning partners? What specific strategies should be used, and why?

4. To what extent is it the responsibility of a faculty member to intervene when students fail to "get along" in the course of working together on interdependent projects? What are the likely actions of intervening versus ignoring the situation?

Summary

Each profile in this chapter is necessarily structured to be open-ended, thereby permitting readers to analyze, reflect on, and consider how they might address similar issues in their own institutional context. We can, however, identify some common themes in these profiles and provide a brief discussion of how to better understand and support adult learners. Some of the *student issues* include clarifying and ensuring that the right resources and solutions are provided to adult learners; assessing the college-equivalent of prior experiential learning of adults; financing higher education for adult learners; and managing assignments, schedules, and peer relationships.

In *Been There, Done That*, learners at St. Mary of the Meadows College are necessarily frustrated in the ambiguities between what they perceive the institution has marketed to them, and in what Flora Hunt and her colleagues are prepared to do in practice. Often, such circumstances can be minimized or avoided with proper coordination and clarification on policies, practices, and procedures concerning adult learning. This requires leadership over adult-centric matters, and communication, training, and ongoing monitoring to ensure that faculty, staff, students, and other stakeholders are aware of the institution's intended actions.

Such explicit approaches to handling adult learning issues is exemplified in *The Case of the Phony Portfolio*, in which Matina Edwards fails to follow the steps and approaches that the college requires, and attempts to get thirty-six hours of credit based on one project that she completed at work. This case also highlights the realities that many adult learners have highly visible, successful lives outside the institution, and they often expect institutional representatives to treat them in a manner similar to how they are regarded in other settings and contexts. Faculty and administrators can treat adult learners with the dignity and respect they deserve while still safeguarding institutional policies and prerogatives. In this particular profile, one useful suggestion would be to build in reviews of student work in milestone increments that allow for early identification of issues, clear and honest feedback to the student, and an opportunity to diffuse or rectify any perceived misunderstandings earlier in the process.

Financing higher education for all learners is a considerable fiscal, policy, and practical issue in higher education. For adult learners such as Allegra Straphos, she truly is in *The Financial Aid Trap*. Clearly, faculty should not be expected to lower expectations for courses based on student involvement in outside activities. In this particular profile, some diagnostic questions are necessary if sound advice can be offered and new courses of actions pursued. For example, does this overwhelming semester represent an isolated incident, a pattern of behavior, or a system issue for the student? Is this student a rare case, or is she fairly representative of several kinds of learners comprising the institution's student body? Depending on the answers to these questions, interventions might range from advising the student on course-taking issues to an examination of alternative forms of financial aid to a restructuring of course offerings (for example, taking one class that meets intensively for eight weeks instead of two that meet for sixteen).

Finally, both parts of *A Student's Dilemma* reflect the challenges inherent in working with other students to complete assignments—issues which, to be fair, are not exclusively in the realm of adult learners. Because learning to work interdependently in collaborative ways is an instructional objective in many courses, simply avoiding student group work is not a feasible solution. Nor can and should faculty be expected to micromanage every student interaction, dispute, misunderstanding, or hurt feeling. Practical suggestions for such cases might include clear performance expectations of students, the ability to evaluate and provide feedback on student-partner performance early and often, structuring graded assignments in such a way that does not disproportionately disadvantage a high-performing individual who ends up with poor-performing or "social loafing" student colleagues, and a willingness for the instructor to listen and intervene in group dynamic issues when warranted.

The *student issues* presented in these profiles are representative of just a few of the many possibilities and eventualities in supporting adult learners. Please refer to the Action Planning and Readings and Resources sections that follow to help you and enhance understanding of these issues in your own institutional context.

ACTION PLANNING

- Based on information presented in the preceding profiles, what are similar *student* issues related to adult learners at your college or university?
- What is your college or university doing especially well to understand and support *student* issues related to adult learners?

- In what ways can your college or university improve its efforts to understand and support *student* issues related to adult learners?
- Where might support for improvement efforts be garnered? To what extent will there be any resistance to such efforts?
- What are immediate next steps? What are longer-term considerations?
- Other resources, suggestions, or ideas?

READINGS AND RESOURCES

The following readings and resources are provided to expand knowledge on a particular *student issue* related to adult learners in higher education. Each was selected because it expands on a concept, idea, or approach highlighted in one or more profiles. A more comprehensive bibliography is included at the conclusion of this book.

Achacoso, M. V., and Svinicki, M. D. (Eds.). Alternative strategies for evaluating student learning. *New Directions for Teaching and Learning, 100.* San Francisco: Jossey-Bass, 2004.

Aslanian, C. B. *Adult students today.* New York: The College Board, 2001.

Bash, L. *Adult learners in the academy.* Bolton, MA: Anker, 2003.

Bash, L. (Ed.). *Best practices in adult learning.* Bolton, MA: Anker, 2005.

Kasworm, C. E. Adult meaning making in the undergraduate classroom. *Adult Education Quarterly, 53*(2), 81–97, 2003a.

Kasworm, C. E. Setting the stage: Adults in higher education. *New Directions for Student Services, 102,* 3–10, 2003b.

Kilgore, D., and Rice, P. J. (Eds.). Meeting the special needs of adult students. *New Directions for Student Services, 102.* San Francisco: Jossey-Bass, 2003.

Merriam, S. B., Caffarella, R. S., and Baumgartner, L. M. *Learning in adulthood: A comprehensive guide.* San Francisco: Jossey-Bass, 2006.

Ross-Gordon, J. M. Adult learners in the classroom. *New Directions for Student Services, 102,* 43–52, 2003.

Thomas, A. M. Prior learning assessment: The quiet revolution. In A. L. Wilson and E. R. Hayes (Eds.), *Handbook of adult and continuing education* (pp. 508–522). San Francisco: Jossey-Bass, 2000.

Wlodkowski, R. J. *Enhancing adult motivation to learn: A comprehensive guide for teaching all adults* (3rd ed.). San Francisco: Jossey-Bass, 2008.

CHAPTER THREE

PROFILES OF FACULTY ISSUES RELATED TO ADULT LEARNERS

The profiles in this chapter cover a variety of *faculty issues* surrounding adult learners in higher education.

In *A Faculty Member's Dilemma*, Brent and Rhoda teach classes that are made up of nontraditional adult students at Ashland University. Patricia Jones-Hemphill is one of their students and, though she seems to be trying her best in the class, she is demanding a lot of time from both professors. She calls multiple times a day, takes up hours for meetings, and doesn't seem to be able to handle things independently. Both professors are trying to be as helpful as they can, but Jones-Hemphill wants assistance and help on every assignment, and every issue that comes up. Brent has set up a meeting to discuss the problems with her, but she sees the meeting as yet another opportunity for Brent to assist her on a project. Something must be done. However, they can't seem to get Jones-Hemphill to see that there is an issue.

Professor Banville, in *A Sheep in Wolf's Clothing*, prides himself on the strict standards he sets, and expects people to adhere to them. Nonetheless, he is lenient when students come to him with a legitimate excuse—but students don't find out that he is more flexible than he appears unless they ask for special accommodations. Although a busy single working mother, with a very hectic life, Monica Hepwood-Morgan insists on doing well and does what it takes to turn everything in on time instead of accepting a late grade. After turning in several assignments and realizing that many students were getting decent grades for late work, she confronts Banville. He is shocked to hear complaints, as most students like his policies. Monica points out that to state one thing and do another isn't right. Thus, Banville ponders the correct thing to do.

Rebellion in the Classroom focuses on Maureen Smithson's well-intentioned approach to teaching management. However, this approach doesn't sit well with all of her students; many find the focus on theory over practice, and didactic instruction over experiential learning, to be a waste of their time. Subtle feedback throughout the semester goes largely ignored by Smithson, until one night several students in the class push back. This affront to the professor's authority is one issue facing Smithson, in addition to determining how she will structure the learning environment to meet disciplinary needs while simultaneously catering to student desires.

Frank Pastore has been an instructor for twenty years. In *Don't They Know I Won the Teaching Award?* it is evident that he has had excellent reviews and is well liked. However, Wes, the associate dean, has been receiving complaints about Frank's teaching. The complaints are coming from adult students who don't think that the teaching style that Frank uses is effective when dealing with adult students. They would prefer that he use a method that doesn't require as much participation outside of class. He does put extra work into his class, but tends to deal with adult students as if they were younger and less able to handle the work. Thus, Frank is conflicted about how to reenergize his teaching in order to deal with this new constituency.

In *I'm Talking About You,* Professor Guran is having a difficult time teaching adult students. Most of his students are working parents, and many of them appear to be "slacking off." They show up late to class with no excuse, turn in late papers, and miss presentations. Their excuses are varied, with most expecting that the reason will be good enough no matter what it might be. After talking with the department head, who offers little assistance, Guran gives the class a case study that demonstrates the problems that arise when a person or group doesn't carry their share of the weight. He pointedly tells them that they are the group represented here, and waits for a response. Some people see the similarity and others don't notice. Will the case study get the students' attention?

Mike is a new teacher at Olympia Career Academy and, in *The New Kid on the Block*, wants some clarity on teaching-related issues. He feels that there is no clear-cut explanation for many classroom situations such as attendance, late assignments, and so forth. Each professor has his or her own way of doing things, which makes it difficult for incoming faculty to know how to do things. Students use the "Well, my other professors . . . " excuse. Mike feels that there should be consistency, which might offend some of the people who have worked there for quite a while.

Profile #6: A Faculty Member's Dilemma (Faculty Issues)

There was a cold wind blowing as Brent Thorpe walked quickly across campus. He had been in the library working, and was now hurrying to get to his office for his scheduled appointments with students. Even after eleven years of teaching, he retained his enthusiasm for the classroom and for his students. He always looked forward to the afternoons when he had office hours because it gave him a chance to work individually with students, and to understand who they were and what their aspirations were. Today, however, he was a little apprehensive because he had an appointment with Patricia Jones-Hemphill. He wasn't sure how to help her navigate the difficult waters of a college curriculum, but he knew that the present situation could not—and should not—continue. When he asked to see her, he had resolved to be candid with her about his concerns, and to offer his assessment of the options available to her. Now that the time of their meeting was imminent, he didn't know how to begin, but he knew that a lot was at stake, for Jones-Hemphill and for himself.

Background

Ashland University is the oldest private university in Birmingham, Alabama, one of the South's most rapidly growing cities. With more than eleven thousand students, Ashland prided itself on the diversity of its offerings, with a range of programs from associate's degree through the Ph.D. For almost thirty years, the University had been actively reaching out to new constituencies, developing off-site, evening, distance learning, and weekend programs. By 2004, over 25 percent of the undergraduate students were nontraditional, and half of the full-time faculty regularly taught in specialized programs or in classes in which nontraditional students were enrolled.

One of the most popular of the University's new programs was its Bachelor of Liberal Studies (BLS) program, designed "for mature students whose prior undergraduate studies had been interrupted, and who were now committed to continuing and completing a degree program." Each year, approximately 150 new students entered the program; the average amount of work at other colleges and universities credited to the BLS degree was forty, leaving eighty-four credits to be completed at Ashland. All entering students were required to take a six-credit course during each of their first three semesters of enrollment. That eighteen-credit course sequence, which had been developed through a FIPSE grant to the University, was titled Issues in Contemporary Life: A Global Perspective. Each six-credit course was team taught by a member of the university's writing and rhetoric faculty, and a faculty member in a social sciences discipline, such as political science, history, international relations, and sociology. There were two educational principles upon which the program was structured: *first*, that returning students would need rigorous training in writing and critical thinking; and, *second*, that student exposure to six different faculty members' perspectives on a unified theme would be stimulating and challenging.

Brent Thorpe had not taught in the BLS program until two years ago, but was enthusiastic about the program, the team teaching, and the students. He received very good evaluations from the students, and developed an excellent collaborative relationship with Rhoda Brandenberg, a faculty member who taught the writing component of the course. A political scientist, Thorpe was open to new approaches to teaching and, for example, had become quite adept at using role playing as a teaching strategy.

This semester, Thorpe and Brandenberg had twenty students in Issues I. At the midpoint in the semester, two students had dropped the course, one for work-related reasons (her company was downsizing and she was being transferred to another city), and the other for unknown reasons, after having attended only two classes. In their third effort at team teaching, the two faculty members were comfortable working with one another, and confident that they had strengthened the course material and objectives over time. They were looking forward to a successful semester.

The First Phone Call

Patricia Jones-Hemphill called Thorpe the day after the first class meeting. A woman "over forty" (as she described herself on the first night of class), Jones-Hemphill was enthusiastic, articulate, and talkative. Even during that first class, Brandenberg had to say once, "Patricia, I think we need to make sure everyone has a chance to speak." When she called Thorpe she said, "I'm so nervous. I've been out of school forever. Do you think I can make it?" Before he had a chance to answer, she continued, "Maybe I should come in and see you. You really need to know more about what I've done. I've even written some short stories. Do you think I should send them to Dr. Brandenberg? Do you know her phone number? I haven't bought the books yet. How late is the bookstore open?" Thorpe smiled as the questions poured forth, without any pause for him to respond. First week jitters, he thought to himself. When she stopped talking, he tried to answer as many questions as he could. Jones-Hemphill said, "Well, I'm sure there's a lot more I will think of to ask you about. I tell you what. I'll call again tomorrow."

A Student with Many Needs

By the end of the third week of class, Thorpe had lost track of the number of phone calls he had received. Brandenberg, too, felt that Pat was taking up a lot of her time. One incident in particular illustrated how time consuming and demanding Jones-Hemphill could be. Brandenberg posted a schedule outside her office door, so students could sign up for appointments in thirty-minute time slots. Pat had put a diagonal line through three consecutive time slots, and left a note saying, "I could NEVER talk about everything that's on my mind in half an hour!!"

In one of her phone calls to Thorpe she started to talk about the stress of working, maintaining a household, and going to school. She said she felt overwhelmed, and started to cry. Thorpe said, "Pat, take it easy. Lots of people feel these pressures. The university has an excellent counseling center, and I know they could help you deal with this problem." "Oh, Professor Thorpe," she said, "I could never talk to a stranger. I'd really like to explain all of this to you." He agreed to talk to her, and they spent over an hour in his office one afternoon before class.

During week six of the course, a ten-page library research paper was due. Jones-Hemphill had changed her topic twice, and for three classes in a row she asked questions at the beginning of the class, delaying the start of the day's topic. Brandenberg said to Thorpe after class, "I guess this is better than having her call us two or three times a day." She was smiling, but Thorpe sensed that she was annoyed. The next day, Thorpe received a call from the head of the reference department of the library. He said that Jones-Hemphill was "charming," but didn't seem to understand what services the reference desk staff could provide, and what was "excessive." "We simply aren't equipped to handle one-on-one work for several hours at a time." Thorpe called Pat and asked her how her paper was coming.

"I'm glad you called," she said, "because I'm just overwhelmed. Everyone has told me different things to do. Also, we have relatives coming from out of state this weekend, and I just won't get the paper in on time. I have an idea. I'll send you a draft, and you can read it, and I'll rewrite it in a week or two." Thorpe said that missing the deadline was a problem and that extensions were not permitted, except for medical reasons. "I have high blood pressure," she responded, "and I can get my doctor to call you." Thorpe decided not to pursue the issue further because he had already been on the phone for fifteen minutes, and other students were waiting to see him.

She came thirty-five minutes late to the midterm, rushing into the room, saying, "What a day at work. It's unbelievable. I didn't even have lunch today." When the allotted time for the exam was over, she went to Brandenberg, who was supervising the exam, and said, "I get so nervous when I have to write. I absolutely need another fifteen minutes." Brandenberg initially said "no" but relented when Pat grabbed her hand and said, "I'm pleading with you. I'm trying so hard." The next day Brandenberg called Thorpe. "Brent," she said, "we're not being fair to the other students by spending so much time and making so many exceptions for Pat. You've got to talk to her!" Thorpe knew she was right, and at the beginning of the next class, he asked Jones-Hemphill to meet with him. "I'd love to," she said. "I went to a session at the Learning Center on study skills and I didn't understand all of it. I'll bring the handouts, and you can explain them to me."

Jones-Hemphill was fifteen minutes late. "My youngest child is dyslexic," she said, "and I went to the Education Department to find someone to talk to, but everyone was busy." "Pat," Thorpe said, "we have some issues to discuss."

QUESTIONS FOR CONSIDERATION AND DISCUSSION

1. What responsibility do faculty members at Ashland University have to continually meet with Patricia Jones-Hemphill? If you were Brent Thorpe how might you handle this situation?
2. What approaches should an institution have for dealing with students such as Patricia Jones-Hemphill? How might this situation have been avoided? How can a faculty member prevent one student from monopolizing the class and instructor's time?
3. What are the concerns of the student in this case? In what ways, if any, should the faculty member intervene?
4. What are the concerns of the faculty in this case? Why and how should these concerns be addressed?

PROFILE #7: A SHEEP IN WOLF'S CLOTHING (FACULTY ISSUES)

The student looked calm and composed, but Walt Banville could see the tension in her eyes and in how stiffly she held herself. Something is really troubling her, he thought, but instead of asking her about it directly, he said, "Monica, you said that you needed to see me as soon as possible, so tell me, what's wrong?" She looked at him, began to say something, hesitated, and then started again. "Professor Banville, how much do you know about me, my major, what kind of jobs I have had, what my goals are? Do you feel that you understand me and my complicated life?"

Banville paused before answering. Monica Hepwood-Morgan appeared to be in her early forties, and was taking his course in computer security issues. This was the first course she had taken with him, but he knew from the class questionnaire he asked students to complete that she was in her junior year, majoring in economics, completing a Computer Technology certificate, and working to complete a B.S. From comments she had made in class, he knew she worked for Steadfast Financial Bank, the largest bank in the area, but he didn't know what kind of job she had at the bank.

He also recalled hearing someone in the class ask her how her daughter was, so he knew she had at least one child. He said, "I know a few things about you, that you are an economics major and getting our Computer Tech certificate. I know you participate in class, and your work so far this semester has been good. Is there more you want to tell me? Is there a specific issue you want to discuss?"

"Professor, I'm a hard-working student, and all my other instructors will tell you that. You have a reputation as being one of the best teachers in the department, and I kept hearing about how much students liked and respected you. So I enrolled in this course thinking that we would get along just fine, but . . . ," she paused, struggling, "but I really think you are unfair and you say one thing and mean another. You set up rules and then ignore them. You set up deadlines that people don't pay attention to because you don't. I followed the rules and met the deadlines, and other people just do what they want and you don't penalize them for being late, or give me extra credit for being on time."

Banville was taken aback by her statements and the intensity she obviously felt. "I try to be flexible because I know that many students have other responsibilities, jobs, family, other things," he said. "Isn't flexibility on my part something students want?"

Hepwood-Morgan looked at him coldly. "Some students may want that, but I want clarity and an honest statement of what I need to do. To sound strict in class and then let any excuse be the basis for making an exception is unfair to students like me who accept the rules even if it's difficult to do that."

Banville started to defend his practice of approving late submissions, but then stammered, started again, paused, and finally said in a quiet voice, "I have never seen it from that perspective before. I have always believed that accommodation on my part was recognition of the complexity of people's lives. You've made some intriguing points here, raised some issues I want to think about. Let's meet again next week, and I will try to sort through these issues."

Hepwood-Morgan did not seem placated by his statement, and said simply, "Well, then, let's make an appointment."

BACKGROUND

Walt Banville had taught at Springfield Valley University since completing his doctorate there nearly fifteen years earlier. In fact, SVU was the only place where he had ever taught, and he was proud of his connection to the university and was fiercely loyal to it. He was respected by both faculty and administrators, served on several university committees, had been an officer of the university senate, and had served a two-year term as chair of the Management Information Systems Department. His courses received above average evaluations from students, and he had been named "Professor of the Year" by the Student Assembly several years before.

It was, however, his role as chair of the "Serving New Constituencies" Committee that he believed had been his greatest contribution to the life of the university. SVU was founded in 1867, just after the Civil War, in Palisades, the second largest city in the state. Palisades was—and is—an important financial, industrial, and transportation center and it became the cultural and financial center of the state, eclipsing both New Hampton, the state capital, and Frantawa, the largest city.

SVU was the flagship higher education institution in the state, attracting many of the best high school graduates in the state, and a growing number of out-of-state undergraduates who chose SVU over public and private institutions in their own states. Because the Health Sciences Campus (which included the Schools of Nursing, Medicine, Physical Therapy, and Veterinary Medicine) was forty miles away, SVU had retained an emphasis on arts and sciences, humanities, and the social sciences. Its master's and doctoral programs in these areas were highly regarded, and some were nationally ranked. The School of Management was the only professional school housed on the Palisades campus, and it had a long tradition of collaboration with other campus programs, and a considerable number of faculty had joint appointments in management and traditional academic disciplines in the university. The state-supported School of Law had been established in New Hampton in 1906.

Enrollments at SVU were strong and its students were academically well qualified; annual rankings of colleges and universities by the news media consistently rated the university as "highly competitive" or "highly selective." Over time, however, the robust economy of Palisades resulted in population growth well above the state median. With that population growth came increased demand for new programs, particularly from part time students. At first, that demand could be addressed by adding additional sections of required and popular courses. By 1990, the under-graduate headcount at SVU was one-third part time, with further increases predicted over the next decade.

The part-time student population comprised mostly older students roughly divided among three groups: older students who had never attended a postsecondary institution, but who were now interested in a certificate or degree; older students who had been enrolled previously, and had accumulated credits (in some instances, even an associate's degree), and now wanted to complete a degree program; and, older students who had an associate's or bachelor's degree, but now wanted certification, advanced training or retraining, or some other employer or professionally mandated educational activities.

As an institution that had served traditional students for more than a century, the University's faculty and administrators were unprepared for the "new" students who were now such an obvious presence on campus. In 1999, the university established a "Serving New Constituencies" Committee, and Banville was named as its chair. The committee made numerous recommendations about how administrative and academic services could be improved to accommodate part-time students, many of whom were employed, and could only take courses in the evenings. It also recommended a simplified procedure for approving certificate programs, making it far easier to introduce new programs. There was some reluctance within the committee to "telling the faculty how to teach" new student constituencies, but there was agreement that some *voluntary* faculty development workshops could be made available.

Because of his service as chair of the committee, Banville was considered to be an advocate for increased flexibility and respon-siveness in the curriculum and in teaching. His courses were popu-lar with older, working, part-time students, and he felt comfortable teaching those students, even though, as he admitted to his col-leagues, "quite a few of them" were older than he was.

Creating the "Right" Environment for Nontraditional Students

In his own courses in the Department of Management Information Systems, Banville saw steady increases in the number of part-time students enrolled, and by 2000 it was not uncommon for some courses to be evenly divided between full- and-part-time students. Many class discussions were enriched by the older, working students telling "war stories" about their on-the-job experiences, and that was very satisfying to Banville. There were, of course, some frustrations as well; it was just about impossible to start the class on time with some student arriving ten, fifteen, or even twenty minutes late. Almost invariably, these were students who worked and were enrolled part-time.

Still, on balance, Banville and many of his faculty colleagues believed that the "mix" of older and younger, full- and part-time students enriched the learning experience. Banville worked hard to maintain reasonable balance between "student accountability." This, however, was a challenge, because there seemed to be an endless array of special circumstances, unanticipated events, and emergencies as students faced obligations and stresses as employees, parents, caregivers, and commuters, and as civic, religious, and community members.

Typically, Banville evaluated his students on the basis of the following:

Two case studies	20%
In-class midterm exam	25%
Group project	25%
Research paper	20%
Class participation	10%

Note: There is a 3 percent penalty for each missed class after two absences. *No exceptions.*

At the first class, he asked students to submit a list of any class sessions they knew they would have to miss. He wrote in the syllabus:

> Include on this list any business trips you will have to take, your son's graduation, your niece's wedding, and your supervisor's retirement party. If you know in advance when you cannot be here, I can try to accommodate your schedule in terms of assigning in-class presentations, or can help you make arrangements to make

up some work you will have missed. Within reason, scheduled business commitments and significant family events will not be included in the "two missed classes without penalty" rule. Missing class is a serious matter. Exceptions to this policy will be reviewed on a case-by-case basis.

The syllabus included a similar statement about late papers and assignments. Students who made arrangements in advance would not incur penalties, but assignments turned in late without having made prior arrangements would be penalized with exceptions considered only on a case-by-case basis. Banville thought his rules were clear and, indeed, there were not very many "exceptions" he was asked to consider each semester. He used to joke with his colleagues that a great many traditionally aged students seemed to have roommates who "accidentally" deleted their papers from the hard drive, and a great many older students had infirm parents who needed to be hospitalized or placed in nursing homes.

Over time, however, the boundaries between what was reasonable and what was not became blurred. What about a water main break in downtown Palisades which caused massive traffic delays and the closing of almost half of the buildings in the downtown area? If a planned business trip was suddenly postponed and rescheduled for another time, did the "advance notice rule" apply to the new dates? If an illness, such as a virus, could be considered as a special circumstance, should the same consideration be given to a computer virus?

SVU, like many other universities, had a long tradition of expecting faculty to make special arrangements for class attendance and assignment deadlines for students participating in university-sponsored activities, such as intercollegiate sports, both of which required considerable travel. Banville thought about this from time to time, and wondered whether it was equitable to make exceptions for those activities, but not make similar exceptions for students who worked full-time and had an obligation to travel in connection with their work. More than most faculty members, he was aware of the principle of "equal treatment" of traditional and nontraditional students. The problem was: *how could you achieve that kind of equity with so many different, compelling, and mitigating circumstances?*

Several years after his hard work on the committee, Banville came to the realization that trying to be responsive and fair to nontraditional learners was more of an art than a science, and that his instincts and intuition served him well when confronted with specific issues and problems. He still used the "class policies" and found them to be useful guides, but he came to rely more on being a "listener" than on being a "regulator."

He still gave his "tough talk" about attendance and deadlines at the beginning of the semester, but, in reality, he was not as tough as he sounded, and he knew that all too well.

A STUDENT IN AN UNFAMILIAR ENVIRONMENT

Monica Hepwood-Morgan was a junior majoring in Economics. She was an assistant loan officer at Steadfast Financial Bank, specializing in the very lucrative mortgage market for condominiums. A single parent, she had two children, a daughter who was eleven, and an eight-year-old son. She was taking Computer Security Issues because she knew that at her next promotion at the bank she would be responsible for merging mortgage records from two banks which had recently been acquired by Steadfast as well as for any future mergers which might occur.

Hepwood-Morgan led a hectic and fast-paced life. Unlike some of her friends who said they were "living at the edge" with no room to maneuver, she felt that she could manage her responsibilities and commitments IF she could remain organized. She was a list maker, and began and ended each day marking off the tasks she had completed, and writing down the new ones. She allocated her time carefully among her three major activities: her job, her children, and her education. With flextime at the bank, and with a network of baby-sitters, supervised activity groups and sports, and help from her mother and sister, she had been able to take two courses a semester at SVU, and was making good progress toward her degree.

There were complications, of course. Her daughter had a severe case of asthma, and in the past year there had been several times when she had to leave work early (or even miss a day entirely) because of her daughter's illness. Her mother, in her seventies but still in good health, had begun to experience "panic attacks" if something unexpected occurred. A few months ago, her mother locked her keys inside her car at a shopping mall, and became so unsettled that Monica had to leave work and go to her mother's aid. The previous spring, Monica had been invited to enroll in the honors sections of one of her economics courses, but had to decline because the course met in the middle of the day, and she knew she couldn't be away at the times when the class met.

Nevertheless, she felt that she was in a better position than many to be able to handle her multiple commitments. Getting a degree was doable, she thought, if she planned her time carefully. She mapped out the assigned work for each course carefully, dividing the reading assignments into "daily quotas" and preparing written assignments so that she had at least two or three days between completing the rough draft and writing the final draft. If she found that two assignments were due on the same day she set her schedule to complete one of the assignments a few days early. When she had long or difficult reading assignments, she would sometimes make a copy of the assignment so she could carry it with her to work, and perhaps have time to read during her lunch break, or when she was waiting for a meeting to begin.

When she enrolled in Banville's course, she realized that she did not know a single student, because this was the first MIS course she had taken. Many of the students appeared to know each other, and when Banville entered the room it was evident that many students already knew him, and he called some of them by name. He reviewed the syllabus, explained his policies about grading, attendance, late papers, and then listened attentively as each student made a brief introduction describing interests and goals.

She enjoyed the class lectures and discussions, and found the readings to be very interesting. The first written assignment was difficult, and she realized that she hadn't allocated enough time to do an excellent job. She thought about taking a day off from work, but she had missed a day the previous week because her son had the flu, and things were piling up. So, she came to class with the paper finished, but not really at the level she wanted. She took her usual seat next to a woman who looked about her age, and who had a daughter in the same grade as her daughter, so they had gotten to know each other a bit. Monica said, "That was a tough assignment. I needed twice as much time as I had." Her colleague said, "Is it really that hard? I'll have to remember that." "You mean you haven't finished it? What will you do?" Monica asked. The woman said, "I'll get to it next week when my husband is back from his trip and my life is a bit more normal. With five kids, no spouse, and other classes on my mind, something had to give."

Monica was surprised that someone would be so willing to accept a late grade penalty, but didn't say anything. When the papers were returned by Banville the following week, she noticed that three or four students did not get their papers back, and thought that perhaps he hadn't finished grading them.

Several weeks later, she was to give a ten-minute oral presentation on behalf of the group she was working with on their project for the semester. The schedule for the group presentations had been assigned during the second class meeting. As the presentations were about to begin, Banville said, "We're only going to have three reports today because Chris tells me that his group isn't quite ready for prime time." People laughed, and Chris made a gesture of looking very ashamed, to everyone's delight. After class, Monica sought Chris out and asked him whether his group would be penalized for being late. He replied, "Nope. We explained that we could give him a lousy report today, or a better one next week, and he told us to go for quality. What a relief that was." Again, Monica was surprised because Banville's rules seemed so clear, but she decided not to say anything.

As the midpoint in the semester approached, Hepwood-Morgan was apprehensive about the literature review she had to submit as part of her research project. She had never done a literature review before, and found herself unsure about how to select some works and eliminate others. It seemed that the more she looked, the more she found, and her list got longer, not shorter. The literature review was due the following Wednesday, and she decided she had to take Tuesday off as a personal day, even though she was very busy at work with several important deadlines approaching. Over the weekend, however, her carefully organized world began to show some cracks and strains.

"It's Done, But it's Not Very Good"

On Saturday, her son and his best friend had a "skateboard showdown" in her driveway. Five hours and seven stitches later, she was too tired and too stressed to get much work done. On Sunday, her mother called from a shopping mall, and was distraught. She had been in a hurry, and had locked her keys in her car with the engine running. Monica could tell her mother was having an anxiety attack, and she knew from past experience that she needed to get to her mother and calm her down. When she returned home several hours later, she had to face the fact that she had accomplished very little on her literature review, and it was due in three days!

On Monday, her supervisor stopped by and said that even though she had requested a personal day, she was really needed at a noontime meeting because she was the most knowledgeable person about a particular condominium development where the bank had significant financial commitments. "It will only take an hour, two at the most," her supervisor said. Monica knew that she could be helpful at the meeting, and she agreed to be there. More time allotted to the literature review was gone!

At 3:00 AM on Wednesday morning, she had a draft completed. It's done, but it's not very good, she thought. She wondered whether she should risk an automatic penalty and hand it in late, but decided that she would just have to take her chances, and so she handed in the paper in class Wednesday evening. Once again, it was obvious to her that the pile of papers was smaller than it would have been if every class member had submitted a paper.

At the end of class, a student she had chatted with a few times asked her if she handed in her paper. Monica nodded, and the student said, "Do you mind if I ask how many references you had? I'm hoping to finish my paper by Friday, and just want to get an idea of what I should be aiming for." Monica decided to ask her why so many people ignored the strict class rules. The student smiled and said, "I have taken another course with him, and—trust me—his bark is worse than his bite. He believes in deadlines and student responsibility, but if you tell him the truth, he really understands that a lot of us work and have other responsibilities."

"But," Monica said in exasperation, "I didn't know, no one told me. I just read the syllabus and listened to what he said. You mean I could have had more time on this paper?" The other student said, "Look, I'm sorry you didn't know, but to tell you the truth, I like his approach. He sets high standards, but he is responsive if people approach him with legitimate reasons for being late, or missing class."

Confronting the Contradiction

Driving home from class, Hepwood-Morgan felt her anger growing. Had she known, she might have made different choices about handing in her assignments. She wished she had asked more questions of other students, but, she thought, how could I have known that there was a contradiction between what Professor Banville said and wrote, and how he actually responded to student requests? She pondered how much stress she had felt to complete the literature review on time, and she thought about how certain she was that the paper was not as good as her usual work, and how much better it could have been IF . . . .

Practical and pragmatic, as always, she decided that she wanted to meet with Banville and tell him of her frustration and anger. It won't change anything, she mused, but at least he will know how this has affected me. When she got home, she sat down in front of her computer without taking off her coat. She sent an e-mail to Professor Banville asking to see him as soon as possible, indicating that she would even take time off work to do so.

A week later, Hapwood-Morgan and Banville sat facing one another again. She was waiting for him to begin, wondering if he would be conciliatory or defensive. He began, "I have given a great deal of thought to what you asked me about last week. I am very sorry for your distress, and I wish I could make you feel better, but at this point I doubt that there is anything I could say that would appease you. Sure, you can rewrite any of the papers you want, and you can have extensions on the remaining work. That's easy for me to do. But I want you to understand that there is a larger issue at stake here, involving the need to set high standards, and to expect students to meet those standards, but maintaining flexibility as individual needs arise. Tell me honestly: would you rather be in a course where the bar was set high or in one where 'anything goes'?"

Questions for Consideration and Discussion

1. What are the *student* concerns in this case? What is the basis for those concerns?

2. What are the *faculty* concerns in this case? What is the basis for those concerns?
3. How could this situation have been avoided? What policies and approaches might have been able to keep a student from these problems?
4. How much influence should one student's problems have on a teacher's method or course polices? What should an institution do about situations such as these, and what changes might you suggest?

Profile #8: Rebellion in the Classroom (Faculty Issues)

The clock on the wall at the front of the classroom indicated 8:45, five minutes after the class was scheduled to end, but no one had moved to get up and leave. The air was filled with tension: two women seated alongside one another were in tears; one man was whispering urgently to another, as if trying to calm him down; and the faculty member, Maureen Smithson, was clutching the sides of the lectern, almost as if it were a lifeline. A well-dressed man seated in the front row looked around and said softly, "Professor, what should we do? Is the paper still due next Tuesday, or will you make a change? I can't speak for anyone else, but I'm confused. I listened to the arguments, and I agree with some of them, and disagree with some of them, but most of all I'm worried about getting a good grade. I just can't afford to screw up or waste my time." Students around the room slowly nodded their heads, affirming what he had said. Now all eyes were on Smithson.

Background

Maureen Smithson was a professor of management at Monroe University, a large, public, urban university located in downtown St. Louis. She taught courses in the popular MBA program, as well in the undergraduate major in management. When Smithson arrived at the university in 1987, most of the undergraduate courses in management were offered during the day, but gradually evening and weekend classes were added, and by the mid-1990s, only half the courses offered were taught during the day. This shift reflected changes in the university's demographics; by 1990, 40 percent of undergraduate students and 70 percent of graduate students were registered on a part-time basis. Included in those numbers were university personnel, taking advantage of the generous tuition benefits to employees. Management, communications, and public administration were the most popular undergraduate majors.

Smithson was one of several faculty members who taught Principles of Management, a required course for undergraduate management majors, and a prerequisite for many advanced courses in the program. Faculty teaching the course usually met once to talk about how they would organize the course, but there was no requirement that all of them cover the same material, or use the same texts. Smithson used a well-respected text, *Fundamental Issues in Contemporary Management*, and she almost always used the same types of assignments: an exam at the last class session, covering the readings (25 percent); an unannounced quiz based on the reading assigned for that class (15 percent each); a research paper comparing various theories about a particular management subject, such as performance appraisal or strategic planning (35 percent); an analysis of an article from a designated management journals (15 percent); and class participation (10 percent). Her teaching evaluations were respectable, with her overall rating of 4.1 (out of 5) placing her just ahead of the 3.9 average for all management faculty.

From Smithson's perspective, this semester's class had been routine. She had given the unannounced quiz on planning and managing information systems, and the grades were low. A few students complained in class that an unannounced quiz was unfair because not everyone had time to read the assignments before class. She replied that it was in the syllabus, and that as managers they would all have to be prepared for "whatever comes along." In addition, throughout the semester a group of students were interested in class discussion, frequently asking questions as she lectured, or making statements such as, "That reminds me of something I had to deal with at work." Finally, Smithson said to the class, politely but firmly, that with so much material to cover there wouldn't be time for anything but brief questions and discussions. Halfway through the semester a woman who worked at the university, and who was planning on being a management major, raised her hand at the beginning of class and said: "Professor Smithson, one of my friends is in another section, and they break into small groups every week to discuss how the reading assignments relate to their own experiences. Could we do that too?" Again, Smithson handled the situation calmly by describing her philosophy of teaching: "You need to know what the important researchers have said, and when you understand that well, there will be time for you to relate their ideas to yours. This is not the course to do that in."

THE INCIDENT

With a month remaining in the course, Smithson came into class and distributed the assignments for the analysis of the article. Each student was given the name of the author, title, and journal issue for analysis. She said that she made specific assignments rather than giving students choices because she didn't want students covering the same material they had written about in their research papers. As she spoke, she saw a range of emotions in her students' faces: some looked worried, some looked angry, some just stared at her. Then she noticed a few people start whispering to one another. Something was amiss, but she decided to go on with her prepared lecture, and turned to write some things on the blackboard. Then it happened!

"Wait a minute," someone shouted in a hostile tone, "you can't treat us this way." It was the woman who had raised the issue of small-group discussions earlier in the semester. As Smithson turned around the student continued. "We're not in junior high, and you can't shove assignments down our throats as if you know everything and we know nothing." She looked at the paper she had been given with her assignment on it. "If I want to know about 'How Managers Control Marketing Costs,' I'll read it on my own. In two months I'm going to start supervising two people, and *that's* what I want to read and write about."

Before Smithson could reply, an older woman who had never said a word in class before stood up and said, "I think you are very disrespectful to all of us, Professor Smithson. You come in here every week and don't know a thing about us. I've been the chief teller at the First Commercial Bank of St. Louis for nine years, and I know more about information systems than the officers do, but you don't know that, and you don't care that I could tell about real problems and real solutions instead of reading this dry and lifeless book." She sat down, trembling.

A firestorm of anger erupted. Another student stood up. "My friend Ed here," he said, pointing to the man sitting next to him, "has coffee with me before every class. He's been a manager, and he knows a hell of a lot. He's tried to talk a few times, and all you do is nod and say we have to move on. Move on? That's what we here for, to move on in our careers, and to do that we need some practical examples, not some hocus-pocus 'theory x and theory y' that will not help us one bit." He slammed his textbook onto his desk. Students were nodding their heads and murmuring softly to one another.

Smithson looked out at the faces of her students. Controlling her voice, she said, "I regret that some of you are upset, and I hope after you hear my reasons for conducting the class this way you will feel better. Management is a discipline, and my job is to teach you to be effective as managers. This isn't something like riding a bike where you can learn it by trial and error. To be a manager, you *must* know theory, and when you know theory, you can think about practice."

"Isn't some kind of middle ground possible?" another student said. Judging from his appearance, Smithson thought he was the oldest student in the class; she knew that he was a retired army sergeant now studying for a degree. "Couldn't you let us choose our own articles for this next assignment? I know that I intend to pursue a career in human resource management, and it would help me to be able to read and write as much as I can about that subject; you're asking me to write about strategic planning. Look around the class; most of us work, and some of us have worked for more years than you have. That should count for something. Cut us some slack."

Smithson was shaking her head negatively as he spoke, and then began, "You must understand that as the teacher, I . . . ." "Don't start with another speech," someone interrupted. "I'm fed up, and here's what I'm going to do. I'll do the assignment, but I'll pick my own topic to read about, and if you want to flunk me, that's fine. I'll go right to the dean, and maybe to the president. I know my rights." He reached into his briefcase, took out the university course catalogue, opened it, and said, "The description of this course says 'students can pursue management issues of interest in depth,' and you're not letting us do that." He looked around the room and said, "How many of you will do the same thing and pick your own article to read and analyze?" Slowly, about half the class members raised their hands.

Smithson had never encountered a situation like this before. This was a classroom rebellion. She knew that one issue was her authority as a teacher; she knew, too, that some of these students were mature, experienced, and focused, and that perhaps some flexibility would be beneficial. Most of all, she understood that in order to retain her authority with the students she would need to make a thoughtful decision and do the best she could to make this a learning experience for her students. She said, "Any experienced manager will tell you never to make decisions in haste. I'll think about what you have said, and give you my response in the next class. Now let's all go home and try to put this in perspective."

QUESTIONS FOR CONSIDERATION AND DISCUSSION

1. What are the *student* concerns in this case? What is the basis for those concerns?
2. What are the *faculty* concerns in this case? What is the basis for those concerns?
3. How could this situation have been avoided? What policies and approaches might have been able to keep a student from these problems?
4. How much influence should one student's problems have on a teacher's method or course polices? What should an institution do about situations such as these, and what changes might you suggest?

PROFILE #9: "DON'T THEY KNOW I WON A TEACHING AWARD?" (FACULTY ISSUES)

The voice mail message was short and cordial: "Hi Frank, it's Wes Collins calling. I know there is a meeting of the curriculum committee on Thursday, and I wonder if you would have time for a cup of coffee after the meeting. I'd like to catch up with you, and there's also something I want to discuss with you." Frank Pastore immediately returned the call, and said he'd be delighted to meet his old friend for coffee.

Collins and Pastore had joined the psychology department at Parker University a year apart, more than twenty years earlier. They had worked closely together as colleagues, coteaching seminars from time to time, and were frequent lunch companions in their early years at the university. Several years earlier, Collins had become associate dean of the Arts and Sciences College, while Pastore continued his full-time teaching, concentrating on introductory and intermediate courses for undergraduate students.

When they met for coffee, they exchanged pleasantries and talked about mutual friends. Finally, somewhat awkwardly, Collins said, "Frank, I need to talk to you about something really important which we need to work on together before it gets completely out of control." He paused. "It's about your teaching."

BACKGROUND

Parker University, where Collins and Pastore are employed, lies just beyond the "triangle" of downtown Pittsburgh. A decade earlier, the university began a successful program for working adults named ALT (Adults Learning Together) With nearly two hundred new students starting each year, ALT is appealing to students, and is profitable for the university. Students, whose median age is thirty-eight, enroll in the first twelve credits of the undergraduate program as a cohort and then take the remainder of their coursework in classes open to all enrolled students, regardless of age, work status, or experience. There are four three-credit ALT cohort courses: Critical Writing & Thinking; Learning from Experience; Self Assessment & Career Development; Research, Reflection, & Creativity

As part of his annual workload, Pastore normally teaches one or two sections of two courses popular with ALT students: Theories of Psychology; and Individuals, Couples, and Families. Enrollments in each section averaged about thirty, with between a third and half the students coming from ALT.

"Frank," Collins began, "a group of four students from your Individuals course came to see me with a petition signed by seventeen ALT students complaining about your teaching, saying they aren't learning anything, and that you don't respect them. There have been similar incidents in each of the past three semesters which we ignored, but the complaints this time just can't be dismissed." Pastore was stunned—and hurt. He worked hard in the classroom, took pride in learning every student's name, prepared his lectures carefully, punctuating them with examples drawn from current events and the popular culture, and he was a virtual fixture in the Student Union, always having a cup of coffee before each class he taught so that students would know where and how to find him if they wanted to talk. The fact that there were organized complaints about his teaching was appalling.

Pastore looked intently at his colleague. "Wes," he said, "this can't be true. You've seen me teach. You know how hard I work. What do they mean? What do they want? Don't they know I won a teaching award?"

Collins was sympathetic. As associate dean, he was the administrator who handled complaints from students, including grievances about grades, allegations of racist and sexist statements and behavior, disapproval of attendance or grading policies, and, increasingly, frustration and anger about the classroom performance of faculty members. Privately, Collins thought that students were overly critical of faculty, sometimes preferring entertainment over substance, but his public demeanor was to listen attentively; he had an excellent reputation across the University for treating students seriously and following through on complaints that were brought to his attention, even if he could not always resolve them. He was aware of the significant differences between the university's traditional and ALT students. ALT students were considerably older than the traditional students, more than 70 percent of them studied part-time, 85 percent of them worked full-time, and a survey of recent graduates indicated that only 10 percent indicated that they had received financial support from other members of their family.

Although ALT students accounted for only 25 percent of total head count enrollments at the University, there were some academic programs, majors, and courses, such as those Pastore taught, in which ALT enrollments were quite sizable. Pastore's problem, Collins thought, was predictable and inevitable. He had built his teaching career by targeting the needs and interests of traditional students. He was an avid reader, for example, of the campus newspaper, and often made reference to campus events in class. During his Individuals, Couples, and Families course, he hosted occasional "let's talk" sessions for undergraduates who were in serious relationships. Knowing that almost a quarter of Parker University's undergraduates went on to graduate school, he devoted two class sessions to "test-taking skills" for those taking the GREs. "So much of what Frank does well," Collins thought, "is irrelevant to what ALT students came here to do."

Changing Student Needs

Collins chose his words carefully. "Frank, you need to see this from the perspective of the ALT students. They have different needs than the students you've been used to, and they think you're not responsive to who they are and why they're here." Pastore responded, "Listen to you. Am I supposed to take a poll of what students want? I'm the teacher, I know the subject matter, and I'm not going to change a successful teaching approach just because of a few malcontents."

Pastore's rhetoric was forceful, but even as he spoke, he knew the problem was real. For the most part, his ALT students were hard working and congenial, and he knew that the complaints were not made by "malcontents." The problem *was* real; he had been a teacher far too long not to recognize the signs of restive, disengaged students, and he was aware that the number of ALT students who took a second course with him was small. It was easy to ignore those troubling signs, and to focus on his popularity with traditionally aged students. He spoke again: "Wes, we've known each other a long time. It's not me. The ALT students just don't appreciate what I know, and how I teach. They rush into class, and rush out again. They keep interrupting the lectures with questions, and they constantly take up class time talking about their own experiences. They don't attend any of the special sessions I organize, and they don't utilize the supplementary services I have worked very hard to provide, like online articles and websites I include in the course management system, extra study sessions before each exam, and having regular office hours. Hell, maybe you should arrange my schedule so that I don't teach *any* ALT students."

"Frank, no one is blaming you or criticizing you. I chose to talk to you rather than having your department chair do it because I think we can attack this as a problem to solve. I remember when we were both novices at teaching, and all the cups of coffee we drank talking about how to be effective and successful with students who were just a few years younger than we were! The fundamental issue here is figuring out how these students are different from the ones you have been used to, and how our teaching needs to change because they have changed. I think I can give you some advice to get you started."

"What can I do? I'm not going to any seminars on 'effective teaching' as if I were a brand new assistant prof."

"Look, Frank," Collins said. "You just told me a bunch of things you've noticed about how the ALT students are different from the ones you've taught in the past. Some of what you observed is very interesting, and I have a hunch you can build on what you know about those students to make their learning more effective. And, frankly, it also sounds as if you have some beefs of your own about ALT students that should be addressed. Why not make a list of all the things you've observed about the ALT students? You and I can then take a look at the list and come up with ideas you can use, and advice and suggestions you can give to the ALT students. Come on, old friend, will you give it a try?"

Several days later, Frank sat at his desk getting ready to focus on this problem. He wasn't sure this effort was going to work, but he had given his word to Wes that he would try. Although he was hurt and disappointed, he started to write a list of all the differences, similarities, and challenges he faced dealing with both ALT students and traditionally aged ones.

Questions for Consideration and Discussion

1. What changes must be made in the presentation of material when dealing with adult students?
2. What must an institution do to make sure that all types of students are dealt with in a suitable fashion? What should be the next step that Frank and the associate dean take?
3. What are the concerns of the students in this case? What is the basis for these concerns?
4. What are the concerns of the faculty in this case? At what level should they deal with the students' complaints?

Profile #10: "I'm Talking About You" (Faculty Issues)

Naran Guran waited for the class to settle down before he began his lecture. The class was scheduled to begin at 6:00 PM, but it was now nearly 6:10 and there were still a few stragglers taking their seats. Guran prided himself on being punctual, and he found it irritating that his students were often so casual about getting to class on time, handing in their assignments by the due date, or showing up for scheduled appointments. Although he didn't take it personally, he felt it was another indicator of how indifferent students had become to higher education. There were, he knew, exceptions, and he enjoyed working with the committed and enthusiastic students who enrolled in his courses each semester.

He knew that today's class was going to be provocative, and he was eager to see how the students would react when they finally understood his real purpose for this class.

Background

Central Georgia State University could be described as a prototype of the modern "magnet" university. Situated in the moderately sized town of Griffin, at the intersection of two interstate highways, CGSU attracted students from three of Georgia's major population centers: Macon, Marietta, and Atlanta. Almost half of all Georgia residents lived within an hour's drive of the university. The student population of CGSU reflected the diversity of the population served by the institution. Nearly 40 percent of students were over thirty, half of all students were part-time, approximately one-third were the first members of their family to be attending a postsecondary institution, and 60 percent of undergraduate students were female.

Sixty-three percent of undergraduate students at CGSU were either moderately or highly nontraditional as compared with the national average of 56 percent. Walking across the campus, one could easily see the diversity: the day-care center operation at peak capacity, the cars crowding the streets and filling the parking lots between 4:30 and 6:00 PM as students came to campus from their jobs, the number of students seeking assistance in the counseling center, and enrolling in workshops on stress reduction and time management.

Both the faculty and the academic programs were "attuned" to the student demographics. A large number of faculty participated in workshops focusing on teaching adult learners, and course schedules were published two semesters in advance, to coordinate their course work with their other responsibilities.

When Naran Guran joined the economics department at CGSU as an assistant professor in 2001, he said that one of the primary reasons he accepted the position was the appeal of teaching older students who had "real" work experience. Because he encouraged his students to share their work experiences in class, there was often lively discussion with many students participating. His teaching evaluations were excellent, and his department chair commended him for his success in the classroom.

DESPITE SUCCESS, AN UNEASY FEELING

As he entered the most recent academic year, however, Guran felt increasingly uneasy about certain aspects of the campus culture, and the behavior of a considerable number of his own students. At first, the unease he felt was not specific, but gradually he understood that he was surrounded by evidence of "slippage." Students came late to class, or left early; papers were submitted late with no explanation given except an occasional "Sorry!" scribbled across the front page; requests to take exams at other times were occasionally made on the day of the exam or even later. He knew that his students had many other priorities and commitments, but it seemed as if their academic work was frequently put on the back burner with a tacit assumption on the students' part that it was OK to do so.

Guran tried to make modifications in his course requirements that would keep students "on task and on track," as he said to one of his colleagues. He added a statement to the syllabus that stated there would be a half-letter grade deduction for each day a paper was late. He also included the following statement about exams: "In-class examinations must be taken on the date indicated unless the student has medical documentation of illness on the day of the exam." He was confident that at least some things would change for the better. To his surprise and chagrin, things got worse. Now he was receiving e-mails and phone calls every day from students who said, "I know what the syllabus says, *BUT*," and then the stories began. Every business, it seemed, had a crisis, every family had a sick member, relatives and pets were dying or dead, and no car could be driven more than thirty miles without breaking down.

Now he was being swamped with pleas and explanations, each one plausible, each one pleading "special circumstances." He didn't want to evaluate or compare the requests; he just wanted students to respect and adhere to the requirements of the course. One evening a student gave him a paper that was a week overdue. He looked at her and said, "Judy, you know I will have to penalize this paper." The student, normally soft-spoken and friendly, gave him an icy response. She said: "Do you want a note from my boss? There was a fire in our Jacksonville office, and I was sent there for six days to help out. Do you think I like being late?"

Two weeks later he received another late paper with no explanation, but with a picture of a baby clipped to the first page. The caption on the picture said: "Kelley Ann, 6 pounds 11 ounces, a bundle of joy, and *my excuse.*"

Guran was also troubled by how many students came late to class, and then had no hesitation about going to where they usually sat, even if it meant disrupting other students, and then whispering to someone with the phrase Guran despised: "Did I miss anything?" One evening, a student came to class forty-five minutes late, missing half of the lecture portion of the session. Guran asked to see the student after class, and said, "I am marking you absent because you missed so much of the class." The student, whose work had been consistently at the B+ or A− level, said: "You have no idea how difficult it was for me to get here at all. Our nanny got sick, I had to leave work early to take care of my children, and then had to make arrangements with three different families to drop off each child at a different place so I could come to class. Surely you wouldn't have wanted me to skip the class entirely. Isn't attending half the class better than not attending it at all?" Although Guran did not reply to the student, he wondered if the student had remembered the concept of "contingency planning" which they had discussed some weeks earlier.

"I MUST DO SOMETHING ABOUT IT"

During the last month of the semester, Guran always devoted several class sessions to individual student reports. Each student was assigned a fifteen-minute block of time to present a summary of the major project for the course, and six presentations were scheduled for each class. At the first class, one student never appeared, and did not contact Guran to say he wasn't coming. At the second class, a student stopped Guran in the hall as he was entering the class and said that her project, which was based on a series of interviews with staff supervisors at the bank where she worked, had not yet received final approval from her supervisor, and she could not present the material without approval. "I'm sure I will be able to present next week, or the following week for sure." So, for the second class in a row, Guran had to dismiss the class early because there was no presenter.

The next morning, he went to see his department chair to express his exasperation, and to say that it was not simply his issue, but an issue for the department and the university. "We do not hold our students accountable, and the time has come for us to say what we mean, and mean what we say." Louise Barnett, the department chair, was both sympathetic and supportive, but she added, "I don't know how much we can do about these issues. You know that we have an ever-decreasing number of full-time traditional students, and, well," she paused, choosing her next words carefully, "they have busy, complicated lives and overlapping priorities, and sometimes we have to accept the inevitable limitations imposed by their multiple responsibilities." Guran was silent for a moment and then said: "You may be right, but I'm not ready to lower my standards and expectations, at least not without a fight. This is a challenge, and I must do something about it."

WHO IS THIS CASE STUDY ABOUT?

At the next class session, Guran wrapped his knuckles against the desk to get everyone's attention and said, "This evening we are going to begin with a case study which I am about to distribute. Please read it quickly so we can begin our discussion." Someone called out, "What about the chapters in the textbook that were assigned for tonight?" He replied, "Just read the case. After we discuss it, you will see the connection to this course." He then distributed "The Case of the Delayed Shipment" (see Exhibit 3.1). After everyone had read the case, Guran led the students through a discussion of the issues, focusing the discussion of the behavior and actions of Blenning and Orrett. Opinions in the class were divided with some students arguing that Blenning was at fault because he wasn't more assertive and aggressive in questioning Orrett when

---

EXHIBIT 3.1:   THE CASE OF THE DELAYED SHIPMENT

The Department of Defense needed to order 100 microprocessor "fault indicator" instruments on a "priority" schedule. Typically, each instrument had the capacity to check the accuracy of 60 hard disk drives daily, a maximum of 6,000 individual disk drives for the total inventory of 100 microprocessors. The DoD quality control plan called for checking its current inventory of approximately 900,000 disk drives. The internal calculation was that even working on a 24/7 basis, it would take 150 days to complete the work. The firm which was awarded the contract, Precision Machinery and Equipment Inc., guaranteed delivery of the equipment by March 1st.

Based on PM&E's assurances, and allowing for some slippage as people learned how to use the equipment, and for inevitable "glitches" that could occur, Department of Defense officials assured the Secretary of Defense that the job would be completed by August 23rd, 175 days from when the equipment was received. The contract was signed on November 4th, giving PM&E four months to assemble, test, and ship the equipment to meet the DoD deadline.

Over the next several months, Major Edward Blenning, the DoD representative, stayed in regular contact with Dennis Orrett, PM&E's senior vice president. Orrett kept assuring Blenning that everything was "on track." Some deadlines slipped a bit; for example, PM&E was supposed to send a prototype model so the Defense Department could begin preparing a training manual. When it arrived two weeks late, Blenning called to ask if there were any problems. "Nope," was the response, "small problem, small delay. Nothing to be concerned about."

Further slippage occurred when Blenning expected to receive a list indicating how many pieces of equipment would be shipped to each of the six locations specified in the contract, but had never arrived. Again, Orrett was reassuring, saying that everything was on schedule, and that "delivery on time was guaranteed."

(*Continued*)

On February 17th, less than two weeks before the agreed upon delivery date, Blenning received a call from Orrett stating that there had been major production delays, and the equipment would not be delivered before March 10th or, at the very latest, by March 20th. Blenning was furious. "How long have you known about this? You have been telling me that everything was OK. What's been going on?"

"Look," Orrett said. "We have had a series of small problems, and each one seemed solvable, and I didn't want to worry you. I knew the important thing was getting everything to you on time, that delivery was what you really cared about. I kept thinking as long as I could deliver, nothing else mattered." Blenning could not control himself. "Of course other things mattered; that's why we set up all those 'benchmarks' and that's why I made the phone calls, so I could know what was happening. I expected you to follow the rules we had established, and because you didn't, we will not be able to meet our obligations to others. How could you do that?"

Orrett continued to argue that the delivery would not be *that* late, and that what really mattered was that "even if it's late, you will get what you want." Blenning retorted coldly, "It's more than getting what I ordered or wanted. It's about sticking to a schedule, and being honest when there are problems." It was clear that these two men were angry, and coming from diametrically opposed points of view.

---

those earlier problems arose. Others felt that Orrett was at fault for being evasive, and for trying to justify his dishonesty by arguing that the only important thing was getting it done, even if later than promised.

Guan pressed the class: Who was "most" at fault? What mistakes had each of the two men made? What was the underlying and unstated issue in the case? The discussion continued. Finally, Guran said, "All right everyone, let's settle down and summarize this case. It all boils down to a single question and that question is"—he paused for dramatic effect—"who is this case about?"

His eyes moved slowly across the room, looking at the students who sat before him. He then said softly: "Think about it. Reflect on it. This case is about YOU."

There was a long and uncomfortable silence, and many students kept their eyes fixed on their desks or books, unwilling to look at Professor

Guran. It was clear that many students understood the point he had been trying to make. Some students looked uncomfortable and angry; a few sat clueless as to what was happening. At long last, Guran said, "We need to talk about this. Many of you are not keeping up with the work, many of you miss deadlines, many of you have the same approach as Orrett does, keeping problems to yourself and then rationalizing that if you get it done, it really doesn't matter. Now, I'd like to hear from you."

Questions for Consideration and Discussion

1. To what extent do you perceive that the issues raised in this case are increasing, or remaining steady? How have institutions—and individual faculty—responded to these issues?
2. What should be an institution's policy regarding absences and excuses? Do the students have any legitimate concerns that need to be addressed?
3. What concerns does the faculty member have in this case? What steps need to be taken so that the issue is resolved?
4. To what extent could this situation have been avoided or minimized? What strategies or approaches would you recommend?

Profile #11: The New Kid on the Block (Faculty Issues)

One of the things Mike Southledge enjoyed most about his job as a faculty member at Olympia Career Academy was getting to the office around 4:00 PM, well over an hour before the evening session started. Carrying his "flavor of the day" coffee, he would sit in the large room, which had eight partitioned sections for faculty members to use as their offices. Mike would just relax and wait to see who arrived, and then begin chatting. He liked the other faculty and enjoyed hearing about the variety of experiences they had had, both professionally and in the classroom. He had recently retired after twenty years as senior medical records administrator at the largest hospital in the area, and was now teaching records administration at the academy, even though he had never taught before. The other faculty came from many different backgrounds and professions, reflective of the six different career programs taught at Olympia.

Mike was intrigued by how different subjects were taught in different ways, and by the ease with which more experienced teachers could adapt what they were doing to fit a particular situation which arose in a class session. He listened carefully, participated when he could, and felt that he was both learning and teaching at the same time.

Today, he was particularly interested in a conversation that two faculty members were having in their classes that quarter. After listening for a while, he decided to join.

FACULTY CONVERSATIONS "OFF THE RECORD"

The faculty members were discussing someone they called "Mary Motormouth." She was one of about twenty students who had begun programs at Olympia the previous quarter. A well-established company in the community had rather abruptly announced a year before that they were relocating to another state, leaving several hundred employees without jobs. The state had stepped in, and was providing support for retraining employees, and quite a few had selected programs at Olympia. The problem, one faculty member said, was that many of them had years of work experience in other areas, and they were always asking questions that were not relevant to the class topics and assignments, and they frequently wanted to repeat stories beginning with "That reminds me of . . . ". Mike had experienced some students like that, and he tried to move the discussion along but some students did not get his gentle hints, and once or twice he had said, "Thanks very much" only to have the student say, "I'm not finished yet." Mike was hoping to hear some ideas and suggestions about what to do.

The other faculty member said, "I've had students like that, but I know how to handle them. I get really frustrated with another type, 'Martin Motionless.'" Martin was described a student who took notes when the instructor was making points from the textbook, but never asked any questions and never participated in the class discussions. In fact, when there were class discussions, which some instructors thought was where some of the most important learning took place, Martin put down his pen, as if it were not necessary or important to take notes on anything except what had been assigned in the textbook. The faculty member said, "I think that part of what is valuable about career education is learning from the other students, and hearing what their interests and concerns are. People like Martin aren't 'pulling their weight.'"

By now, two other instructors had joined the conversation, and one of them, Edna Smith-Hawkins, the instructor who had been at Olympia the longest and who had the reputation of being a very effective teacher, said: "I have some of each of those, and I can tell you how I handle them. But, what frustrates me is having students in my class who think that showing up is all they have to do. They come, they sit there, and when we do class exercises or drills, they just wait and do nothing until I give them personal attention. They don't seem hostile, or resentful of being there, but they seem uninvolved, and I'm tempted to look at them and use my teenage daughter's favorite phrase, 'HELLO, is anyone home?' I have never been able to figure out how to involve them."

Most of the students in Southledge's classes were part of a state-supported program to retrain employees who were left without jobs. Earlier in the semester, he had talked informally with more experienced colleagues about how to handle the "seat warmers," students who came to class but did not participate, and the "silent ones," the students whose first language was not English. Mike was convinced that many of the "silent ones" did not always understand him, or the class discussions taking place in class. He was focusing his attention on those two groups, and thought he was making some progress, but he wasn't sure.

Finally, Mike decided to speak. "I'm new at this, as you all know, but I am very concerned about some of my students who don't appear to understand what I am saying in class. I know from their records that English is not their first language, and I know that when they talk to their friends they speak in their language of origin, rather than practicing their English, but from the looks on their faces when I am speaking, I suspect that they don't always understand me. Their written work is usually adequate, but they may get help with that, or they may spend a lot of time working on it. What I worry about is that I don't know if they understand the class presentations and discussions. I am afraid to say anything because I certainly don't want to offend or embarrass anyone."

He was speaking slowly and cautiously because he didn't want to appear critical of the academy or its students. He said then how much he enjoyed teaching. "It thrills me to look at students and realize they have just learned something they never knew before, something that will help them in their careers. But I worry about some of the students and whether or not they are understanding and learning."

A voice from the other side of the room said, "Well, there you have it." Everyone turned, and saw that Monroe Randall, the academic dean, had entered the room. He greeted everyone, and said, "I've been listening, and you have identified one of the great challenges and—in my opinion—one of the great rewards of teaching in a career education program. *Our challenge* is in the range of students we teach, the different backgrounds and experiences they have, and the variety of goals and objectives they have. *Our reward* is in finding a way to accommodate, encourage, and control all those differences in a single classroom, and sometimes even in a single class period."

Mike was impressed by the clarity of Randall's observations. He looked around the room, saw that others were also interested, and said, "Yes, I know you're right, but how can we do that? We've talked about four different types of students in the last fifteen minutes. Can you give us some idea about how to approach each type of student so that we can have greater control and greater satisfaction in the classroom?" Randall said that the issues being discussed informally were important, and suggested that the upcoming faculty development workshop, one of three held each year, be devoted to a continuation of the discussion begun that afternoon.

THE FACULTY DEVELOPMENT WORKSHOP

In planning the workshop, Dean Randall asked Meryl Rinaldi to facilitate the discussion of "Faculty at Work in the Classroom—Up Close and Personal." Rinaldi was chair of the Medical Records Department at Olympia, and had been at Olympia since "the day after God created the world," as she liked to say. She was experienced and committed, and ran her programs well, monitoring faculty activities, attending classes, and talking to students. The Medical Records Department was the largest of the six career programs offered at Olympia.

"I know that many of you are interested in talking about how we can be most effective in working with different 'types' of students and, of course, all of us have strategies we use, and a long list—a very long list I should say—of what *doesn't* work. But before we get to that, I'd like to start by raising some issues about student performance regarding class attendance and the submission of assignments on time." People around the room nodded. Donna Chapman, a ten-year veteran faculty member, said, "Meryl, for the record, let me say that our basic policy of holding students accountable is reasonable and fair."

Rinaldi smiled at her colleague and said, "We've worked together too long and you know me too well. You know I support our policy." She paused, and then said "but." People looked at her, waiting for her to finish the sentence. Finally she continued, "But even though we have rules and policies, we seem to be having difficulty interpreting and enforcing our own rules consistently. I think you have all met Mike Southledge, our 'rookie.' Mike came to me with an interesting problem. Mike, why don't you describe the situation you told me about."

Mike began: "Well, you all know that I'm the new kid on the block, so please be patient. Sometimes a student comes in five or ten minutes late, sits down, and acts as if nothing is wrong. Sometimes it is fifteen or twenty minutes. A few weeks ago, two students walked in forty-five minutes late. I told them at the end of class that I marked them absent because they missed nearly half the class. One of them started explaining things about baby sitters, traffic, and problems getting out of the house on time. I told her that I was sorry for those problems, but she had a responsibility to be on time. The second student was angry and said, 'My other teachers don't mind if I'm late, as long as I show up. I have a lot of responsibilities.' Do we have a policy about when 'late' becomes absent?"

Several people started to speak at once, and Mike held up his hand, saying, "Wait a second. I'm not blaming anyone, or saying that anyone is doing something wrong. I'm asking for help in understanding how we are going to operate so we are able to give a consistent message to our students." He continued:

And, there is another piece of this puzzle I want to mention. When I give in-class assignments, some students don't hand them in at the end of class. Sometimes I get them the next day, or a few days later, with statements like "I forgot to hand it in" or "I wanted to copy it over so it would look better." Even out of class assignments come in well beyond the assigned date. Last week, one student handed in a paper a week late saying that he needed more time.

A student who was standing near me got furious and said, "What's going on? If I had more time I could have done a better job." I said, "I appreciate the fact that you were prompt," but the student just looked at me and said, "Yeah, I was prompt, but who's going to get the better grade?" What should *I* do, and what can *we* do to make sure we are all on the same page in our adherence to rules and regulations?

Meryl looked around the room and smiled again. "See what happens when you bring in new faculty? You have to explain what you do and why you do it. Seriously, though, let's go around the room and talk about what our practices are, how much flexibility we want to permit, and where to draw the line. I think this is an important discussion to have."

She paused, looking pensive, and then said to her colleagues in the room. "Who would like to begin?" There was a long silence. In his short time at Olympia Career Academy, Mike Southledge had observed many inconsistencies in faculty practices. As he awaited the comments of his more experienced colleagues, he couldn't help wondering how forthright they would be.

QUESTIONS FOR CONSIDERATION AND DISCUSSION

1. What are the concerns of the students in this case? What extra considerations, if any, should be given to working adult students?
2. Determine if your institution has guidelines that must be followed by all instructors. If not, should this practice be implemented? Why or why not? What types of standard guidelines, if any, should be crafted?
3. What is your institution's process for training and developing new faculty? What are the real concerns that both Mike Southledge and the more experienced faculty are presenting?
4. What specific recommendations would you make to Mike and his faculty colleagues?

Summary

Each profile in this chapter is necessarily structured to be open-ended, thereby permitting readers to analyze, reflect on, and consider how they might address similar issues in their own institutional context. We can, however, identify some common themes in these profiles and provide a brief discussion of how to better understand and support adult learners. Some of the *faculty issues* include recognizing differences and unique characteristics of adult learners; establishing clear boundaries and expectations with adult students; aligning teaching styles to meet adult learner needs; and holding adult learners mutually accountable for the process and outcomes of their learning.

Patricia Jones-Hemphill, the student profiled in *A Faculty Member's Dilemma*, provides a good example of how adult learner characteristics and challenges are different from their traditionally aged counterparts. Her busy, complicated life represents the many challenges that adults face when coping with juggling personal, academic, family, work, and other responsibilities. Further exacerbating this issue is the high level of need, reassurance, and support this student seeks from her faculty members. In this case, both Brent and Rhoda, the team-teaching faculty colleagues, are well intentioned and supportive, at least initially, of this student's requests. Over time, however, the demands that they perceive she places on them have caused them to reach their individual and collective limits. What, then, should faculty members do in such cases?

First, faculty should consider establishing boundaries with students early in the semester, often stating the expectations for communication and denoting the scope of individual assistance a faculty member is able to provide. Ensuring that assignments are crafted with sufficient detail, including an anticipation of likely student questions and concerns, can help. This is another way to enhance communication with students. In Jones-Hemphill's case, however, issues of self-confidence and self-efficacy may also be present. Faculty can help students gain confidence by providing opportunities, as appropriate, to demonstrate and receive feedback on learning early in the semester, something especially advisable for introductory courses. They can also provide recommendations to campus-based and other resources for student assistance. Finally, when students become overly communicative and blur boundaries, respectfully discussing the issue with the student can often be a way of reminding students about the scope and limits of a faculty member's role.

In *A Sheep in Wolf's Clothing*, Professor Banville seems intent on holding students to high standards and firm deadlines, yet, depending on the circumstances, is often willing to accommodate legitimate excuses from students. This caused one student in particular to call into question the fairness of such a practice, highlighting the often ambiguous space between being consistent with everyone and providing necessary individual flexibility. One potential solution would be to revisit the "rules" presented to students at the beginning of the semester, and to determine which ones are truly nonnegotiable and which ones will be handled on a case-by-case or exceptional basis. Since most students—adult and traditionally aged alike—will attempt to follow the rules, belaboring every potential eventuality a student might encounter is likely not a good use of time or energy on the part of the faculty member. Instead, setting expectations, explaining why rules or policies are necessary, and creating an environment of high standards that also recognizes the reality of life's circumstances can go a long way toward minimizing students' feelings of unfairness.

Striking the balance between consistency and flexibility is also the theme of *The New Kid on the Block*. In this case, reconciling individual styles of professors with the need to calibrate policies and approaches across multiple sections and classes is the issue. Faculty and administrators are encouraged to determine the extent to which there need to be common approaches to things such as attendance and late assignments. Whether or not there is wide flexibility or overly prescriptive and uniform approaches, this information should be provided to students. In situations where there is divergence in faculty approaches, students should be reminded of their obligation to adhere to course-specific policies.

Negotiating the needs of the discipline and the authority of the professor against the desires of students is one issue at the heart of *Rebellion in the Classroom*. This profile represents a clash of styles between the professor and her class, yet also signals some of the perhaps subtle, missed cues the professor failed to identify before the "meltdown" in the classroom. As in *A Sheep in Wolf's Clothing*, many of the issues could have been avoided if the instructor had more explicitly, clearly, and proactively indicated to students the reasons for a particular teaching style or assignment. Reconceptualizing the teaching-learning approach based on the subject matter, needs, and experiences of the learners is also something this particular instructor might be challenged to consider for the future. Finally, being open to feedback and willing to make learners co-inquirers along with the instructor—especially in a class situation such as the one faced by Maureen Smithson—could conceivably allow for covering the needed material and simultaneously accommodating student interests and tapping into their wealth of experience.

A well-intentioned instructor with a perhaps misaligned approach to teaching adult learners was also the focus of *Don't They Know I Won the Teaching Award?* This profile, in particular, reflects the changes occurring in many institutions—especially those who have become more multigenerational over time—in the composition of the student body. Frank Pastore clearly cares for his students' learning and well-being; however, the styles and approaches he uses are not as salient or valued by adults. There are two levels of recommendations in situations like these. One, the institution can provide faculty with demographic information about student characteristics—and, perhaps most important—with strategies to relate to and engage these students. This can help faculty remain aware of how the student body composition has changed around them, perhaps so slowly and subtly that they may have missed overt cues. The second recommendation focuses on individual faculty members, who are encouraged to be mindful of who their students are, to seek to understand their characteristics and motives for pursuing higher education, and to reflect on their own teaching style and practice. Reaching out to and consulting with colleagues who are similarly teaching oriented—and sharing perspectives and effective teaching strategies—is also recommended. One example of a teaching approach designed to get the attention of wayward learners was highlighted in the profile *I'm Talking About You.* In this situation, Professor Guran is having a difficult time teaching adult students and he uses a case study to demonstrate the problems that arise when a person or group doesn't carry their share of the weight. This type of approach is an indirect way of highlighting student issues while also providing the potential to have insights and transformative learning occur on the student's part.

The *faculty issues* presented in these profiles are representative of just a few of the many possibilities and eventualities in supporting adult learners. Please refer to the Action Planning and Readings and Resources sections that follow to help you and enhance the understanding of these issues in your own institutional context.

ACTION PLANNING

- Based on information presented in the preceding profiles, what are similar *faculty* issues related to adult learners at your college or university?
- What is your college or university doing especially well to understand and support *faculty* issues related to adult learners?
- In ways can your college or university improve its efforts to understand and support *faculty* issues related to adult learners?
- Where might support for improvement efforts be garnered? To what extent will there be any resistance to such efforts?
- What are immediate next steps? What are longer-term considerations?
- Other resources, suggestions, or ideas?

READINGS AND RESOURCES

The following readings and resources are provided to expand knowledge on a particular *faculty issue* related to adult learners in higher education. Each was selected because it expands on a concept, idea, or approach highlighted in one or more profiles. A more comprehensive bibliography is included at the conclusion of this book.

Barkley, E. F., Cross, K. P., and Major, C. H. *Collaborative learning techniques: A handbook for college faculty.* San Francisco: Jossey-Bass, 2004.

Bash, L. (Ed.). *Best practices in adult learning.* Bolton, MA: Anker, 2005.

Braxton, J. M. (Ed.). The role of the classroom in college student persistence. *New Directions for Teaching and Learning, 115.* San Francisco:
Jossey-Bass, 2008.

Brookfield, S. D., and Preskill, S. *Discussion as a way of teaching: Tools and
techniques for democratic classrooms* (2nd ed.). San Francisco: Jossey-
Bass, 2005.

Chickering, A. W., and Gamson, Z. F. (Eds.). Applying the seven principles of good practice in undergraduate education. *New Directions
for Teaching and Learning, 47.* San Francisco: Jossey-Bass, 1991.

Cranton, P. *Understanding and promoting transformative learning: A guide for
educators of adults.* San Francisco: Jossey-Bass, 2006.

Erickson, B. L., Peters, C. B., and Strommer, D. W. *Teaching first-year college students.* San Francisco: Jossey-Bass, 2006.

Fink, L. D. *Creating significant learning experiences: An integrated approach to
designing college courses.* San Francisco: Jossey-Bass, 2003.

Kramer, G. L. (Ed.). *Faculty advising examined: Enhancing the potential of
college faculty as advisors.* San Francisco: Jossey-Bass, 2003.

Kuh, G. D. *High-impact educational practices: What they are, who has access to
them, and why they matter.* Washington, DC: Association of American
Colleges and Universities, 2008.

Kuh, G. D., Kinzie, J., Schuh, J. H., Whitt, E. J., and Associates. *Student
success in college: Creating conditions that matter.* San Francisco: Jossey-
Bass, 2005.

Merriam, S. B., Caffarella, R. S., and Baumgartner, L. M. *Learning in
adulthood: A comprehensive guide.* San Francisco: Jossey-Bass, 2006.

Mezirow, J. *Learning as transformation: Critical perspectives on a theory in progress.* San Francisco: Jossey-Bass, 2000.

Miller, T. E., Bender, B. E., and Schuh, J. H. *Promoting reasonable expectations: Aligning student and institutional views of the college experience.*
San Francisco: Jossey-Bass, 2005.

Ross-Gordon, J. M. Adult learners in the classroom. *New Directions for
Student Services, 102,* 43–52, 2003.

Smith, B. L., MacGregor, J., Matthews, R., and Gabelnick, F. *Learning
communities: Reforming undergraduate education.* San Francisco: Jossey-
Bass, 2004.

Vella, J. *Taking learning to task: Creative strategies for teaching adults.* San
Francisco: Jossey-Bass, 2000.

Wlodkowski, R. J. *Enhancing adult motivation to learn: A comprehensive guide
for teaching all adults* (3rd ed.). San Francisco: Jossey-Bass, 2008.

CHAPTER FOUR

PROFILES OF INSTITUTIONAL ISSUES RELATED TO ADULT LEARNERS

The profiles in this chapter cover a variety of institutional issues surrounding adult learners in higher education.

In *Bait and Switch,* Cascade Valley State College has made it a point to offer classes in two different blocks, AM and PM, to serve both traditionally aged and adult learners. They have recruited students based on the idea that they can work any class into their schedule. However, now that enrollment is down, Cascade Valley has made the decision to cut classes from the PM blocks, thus upsetting several adult students. A meeting with the students is held to discuss the problems. The concerns of the students must be balanced against the competing priorities and resources of the college.

Grant University is experiencing financial difficulty. Regan Edwards is being pressured to find a way to improve the situation, and where to allocate the funds that do exist. He has asked Neal Miller and Kimberly Scott to offer their recommendations. Neal feels that the best way to manage the money is to spend a large amount on recruiting new students, which boosts enrollment and brings in more money. Kimberly feels that it is more beneficial to spend money on support services for the existing students, as she feels the university is better off keeping the students that are already there. Thus, the challenge to recruit, retain, or both, must be confronted.

Alderson State College needs to find a way to make all sections of their classes equally productive and cost-effective.

The off-campus classes are not seeing the ratings that the traditional daytime classes do, and the college seeks to make all classes of the same caliber. The school is seen as a good community partner for offering many noncredit offerings; however, such classes generate little to no revenue. Many, however, see these noncredit classes as a "feeder" that ultimately brings students into the credit-earning classes that earn credit. Bedell needs to publish this information in his report in a fashion that considers all aspects without being filled with jargon that makes the document unreadable.

The Choice Is Yours deals with declining enrollment at Ravenal; especially in the English department, there is a need to reduce the number of faculty. A number of the faculty are tenured, and some of them aren't the most productive instructors. Nethro has been told to either cut back by fifteen employees, or to find a way to offer classes off-site and at various local companies. Nethro feels stuck: the faculty are not going to want to put the effort into developing new programs, but downsizing all of the newest faculty would leave only those who are not the most effective. Which is the better option, and who should make the final decision? Further complicating matters, Fordyce gives Nethro one week to have a plan ready to go.

In *The Bottom Line*, Maybank College is seeing a decline in enrollment as women are increasingly choosing to attend coed universities. The school has improved under Pat Seger's direction, but is still seeing a deficit. Hal is adamant that there must be further changes, or the school may have to close. The English as a Foreign Language program is popular, but isn't breaking even. Thus, Hal demands that something be done, whereas Pat claims that some things are more important than the bottom line.

A Promising Partnership focuses on Polly Jenning, an administrator trying to bring more students into Miles Standish University's liberal studies program. She researched employers to find a potential partner for the program, and identified CIS. This organization provides tuition assistance, and over one-third of its workforce has had little or no college. After many meetings with CIS administrators, an agreement was reached: Miles Standish would offer courses on-site at CIS Headquarters. 240 CIS employees applied for admission, and two years after the program began, an evaluation was conducted. Now the time has come to assess the current and future directions of the partnership.

Profile #12: "Bait and Switch" (Institutional Issues)

Ben Gibbs, the academic vice president of Cascade Valley State College, smiled as he gestured for the three students to take seats at the large conference table in his office. Pointing to four people already seated at the table, he said to the students, "Do all of you know the administrators I have asked to join us?". Sensing that he should make the introductions, he said, "Gretta Henton is the associate dean of students for the Evening Division. Paul Hicks is director of Internships and Placement. Lester Mostimoto is the Registrar, and I imagine you all know Norton Livingston, the dean of the Evening Division. Now, please introduce yourselves."

"I'm Craig Mason, and I'm an MBA student. I am director of the Mail Services Division at Western Mutual Insurance."

"I'm Shanda Jackson, a master's student in the international communications program, and I'm currently working at Olympia Software as a customer service representative."

The last student said, "Paige Henry is my name. I am a lieutenant in the Army, working toward a master's degree in education and certification as a school guidance counselor."

Gibbs then began, "I want you to know how much I appreciate the way you have approached these problems, and I hope that we can cooperate to discuss the problems you have raised, and to work toward some solutions."

"Sir," Lt. Henry said, "it is good of you to arrange this meeting, and we want you to know that however serious the problems are, we want to cooperate if we possibly can, but we need things to improve, and soon."

Gibbs looked at her intently and said, "Well, then, why don't we get started?"

Background

The president of Cascade Valley State College liked to describe the college by saying that it had once been a rural college and became an urban one without any effort whatsoever. And, in fact, that was largely true; the college had been established in 1922 on a tract of land twenty miles east of Portland, Oregon. Over the years, however, Portland's growth was largely eastward, and by the 1980s Cascade Valley's campus was virtually surrounded by Portland's suburban communities, a beltway of high-tech businesses, and the typical array of malls and plazas. Although it had lost much of its bucolic atmosphere, CVSC gained a greatly expanded student base, and considerable community support for its many recreational, cultural, and community-oriented programs and activities. A marketing study done in 1988 indicated that there was considerable potential for evening degree programs given the demographics of who lived and worked near CVSC. In 1989, the college created the Evening Division.

From its inception, the Evening Division was designed to provide the same programs and services as were available to students in the college's day programs. Norton Livingston, the only person to serve as the Evening Division's dean, said in a ceremony celebrating the division's fifteenth anniversary, "Our goal has always been parity and we have always been committed to the idea that if it exists during the day, it should exist at night." The college was one of the first public educational institutions in the state to have extended hours for its administrative offices (typically until 8:00 PM) and its library, labs, and other student support services were generally open weekdays until 10:00 PM (or later) and on weekends.

Although it was initially difficult to implement, the college's academic programs were made available to students whether they studied during the day or in the evening. Three administrative procedures were put in place to help achieve the "parity" to which Livingston and others were committed:

1. All required undergraduate courses were offered in what was called the AM/PM block. The same faculty member, for example, would teach a section of College Writing, or Contemporary Social Thought, at 9:30 AM twice a week, and then teach the same material at 6:30 PM on the same days. Students registered for the course could attend either AM or PM sessions as their schedules permitted. This especially accommodated the needs of homemakers and shift workers,

and quickly became one of the most popular aspects of the Evening Division programs.

2. All academic departments were expected to make teaching assignments so that full-time faculty at all ranks would teach both in the day programs and in the Evening Division. Distribution of Faculty Workload reports were submitted and reviewed annually by the vice president of Academic Affairs. Department chairs were asked to ensure that teaching by part-time faculty not be disproportionately assigned to the Evening Division.

3. In satisfying graduation requirements in the major, departments were expected to offer required courses both in the day program and the Evening Division, or in the transition block, a class time assigned from 4:30 to 6:00 PM each day for classes serving both day and evening students.

Initial Success and Then. . .

Because CVSC started the Evening Division program with a focused purpose, with broad support from the faculty, and with carefully delineated administrative procedures, it had an unusually successful start-up and five years after its first classes were held, there was a headcount enrollment of 675 students. In addition, there were 130 day students who took one or more courses in the Evening Division. The number of students receiving B.A. or B.S. degrees each year grew steadily for several years:

Year	Degrees Awarded
1989	118
1990	137
1991	185
1992	205
1993	213
1994	216

By 1995, however, enrollments had declined somewhat, and so had degrees awarded. This was attributed in part to increased competition (a private university in Portland had begun a "bachelor's completion program" in which students could obtain substantial credit for prior learning through a portfolio process), and in part to changes in the local economy and job market.

Livingston had long favored making the college's three master's programs (in business, communication, and education) available through the Evening Division, and the leveling of undergraduate enrollments made the implementation of graduate programs more of a financial necessity for the Evening Division. The programs were inaugurated in 1997, with a substantial marketing initiative. Despite a flurry of activity and initial interests, the enrollments in both education and business were disappointing, and enrollments in communications were barely at the level deemed to be cost effective by the Office of Enrollment Management.

Livingston was quick to respond, initiating new marketing activities, including the establishment of collaborative programs with several local schools systems, with key business employers, and with Fort Taylor, a nearby Army base with more than four thousand military and civilian personnel. Enrollments grew slowly, and by the summer of 2001 were at the following levels:

Graduate Program	Continuing Students	New Students (Fall 2001)	Total (Projected)
Education	37	11	48
Business	42	13	55
Communication	51	17	68

"The problem," Les Mostimoto had written in a memo to Livingston, "is that we cannot maintain a cost-effective operation with numbers like this. We face two problems. First of all, many of the required courses in each of the programs will not make the minimum enrollment of ten, and we will lose money each time we offer a section. And, second, we are wasting resources by keeping offices open when few, if any, students show up. In April, for example, students coming to the Registrar's office averaged six a week, but we had two staff there each weekday night except Friday. We need to do something."

Livingston discussed the problems and Mostimoto's concerns with Henton and Hicks because he knew that their office operations normally generated a good deal of student "business."

They concurred with Mostimoto's assessment that resources were being wasted. "In fact," Hicks said, "I lost an excellent staff member last month who left because she said she was bored just sitting around waiting for students to show up."

After giving the matter considerable thought, Livingston went to see Vice President Gibbs and said, "I feel terrible about having to retreat from our commitment to equity of offerings and services, but I think if we continue on this way we may jeopardize the entire Evening Division. Perhaps we will be able to reintroduce some courses and services if and when enrollments improve." Gibbs said, "Frankly, I'm relieved that you have come to this decision because I have been hearing some grumbling from faculty members who say that these very small sections are sometimes very ineffective." Together, they decided on a three-part strategy:

1. To offer some required courses only once a year in the Evening Division.
2. To offer some required courses only in the transition block.
3. To keep most offices open only one night a week (instead of four), and to keep a few open two nights a week.

ANGRY STUDENT REACTIONS: "WE THOUGHT WE HAD A DEAL!"

Approximately 170 master's students were affected by these decisions. There was a predictable outcry from students when the *Fall Schedule* was published, and an announcement was made about the changed office hours. What surprised Livingston and his colleagues about the student reaction was that it was most intense from the continuing, rather than the new, students.

One incident with a group of master's students in education was indicative of student dissatisfaction. A required course in that program was the Seminar in Counseling Theory, which had an enrollment limit of fifteen. The *Fall Schedule* indicated that the course would be offered only once in the academic year, instead of twice, as had been the practice. A note in the *Schedule* indicated that the course was being offered in the fall and spring during the day, and that Evening Division students could register for those sections "if their schedules permit."

A group of students wrote a letter to Henton stating that the decision to offer only one section a year would likely mean that their graduation would be delayed. "We thought we had a deal," their letter concluded, that students in the Evening Division were "equal partners with those in the day programs, and that we would be treated fairly. Now we find that preference is being given to the day students."

Concerned, Henton tried to defuse the situation by informing the students that she would do whatever she could to have at least one section moved to the transition block. The students did not appear to be satisfied by her action, and in the end she was unable to have a change made because there was sufficient student demand in the day sections to reach enrollment limits without making a change.

Another incident, this time in the business program, provided further evidence of student anger and dissatisfaction. Students in that forty-eight-credit program were required to complete a six-credit internship in their intended field of concentration after they completed twenty-four hours of coursework. When it was announced that the internship and placement office would only be open two hours a week, some students reacted with fury. A petition was sent to Paul Hicks, and he decided to have an open forum to explain why the decision was made.

He spoke about the enrollment and financial problems, and expressed his personal view that the entire Evening Division program might be in jeopardy at the graduate level unless some economies could be achieved. "That's not our problem," one student shouted. "That's your problem. You encouraged us to apply here, you got us to enroll, you made promises to us, and now you're saying 'sorry, we don't have all those things anymore.' Well, at those sleazy discount stores downtown they call that 'Bait & Switch.' You promise them anything to get them in the store, and then tell them you don't have what they came there to buy."

Livingston went back to Gibbs to report on the student dissatisfaction, and to ask for more resources so that the cutbacks could be restored. He expressed concern that unless something was done, students would drop out, or not enroll, and that the financial crisis would be made even worse. Gibbs was sympathetic but was not inclined to do anything. "Maybe I've been an administrator for too long, but I think it is a bad precedent to be too knee-jerk reactive to student issues. Unless we decide that we made a bad decision, we should move forward, implement the plan, and then evaluate its positive and negative consequences later. In addition, we are stretched pretty thin at this point, and it isn't fair to the day students to 'squeeze' them just to honor a commitment made at a time when there were greater resources and more demand."

Things appeared to be at an impasse as the fall semester approached, and then Gibbs received a letter from three graduate students. They described themselves as the "representatives" of students in each of the programs, and said that they were committed to a "reasonable and rational process" and wanted to discuss both the process by which the decisions had been made, and the options which might be possible at this juncture. "We understand and respect the reality that there are constraints," the letter said, "and we want you to understand the negative impact on students of these decisions." Gibbs agreed to convene a meeting, doing so with apprehension because he thought that there was merit to both positions, and knew that, in reality, there were few realistic options.

Gibbs looked around the room. He turned to Livingston and said, "Nor, why don't you review the situation for us, describing how we got to this point, and then let's have these three students tell us what they think, and what they think we should do."

Questions for Consideration and Discussion

1. To what extent are the evening students' concerns about access and "parity" legitimate? What could Cascade Valley State College have done to avoid this situation in the first place?

2. What challenges are faced by institutions that seek to simultaneously serve both full-time (day) students and part-time (evening) students? What opportunities are present, as well?

3. What advice would you provide to Ben Gibbs in order to satisfy student issues in the short term? What are the longer-term issues and strategies that Ben and his team must confront?

4. To what extent are emerging technologies and pedagogical practices making situations like those described in this case less likely to occur in the future? How might institutions and individual faculty respond to these changes?

PROFILE #13: GRANT UNIVERSITY (INSTITUTIONAL ISSUES)

Regan Edwards paced in his office as he tried to sort out the issues he needed to deal with in the next several days. As the dean of Continuing Education at Grant University, Edwards was responsible for planning and implementing continuing education programs at the university; over the past three years he had felt pressure from the president to expand offerings, and to increase the revenue produced by his division. He had been very successful in attracting faculty members from other divisions to teach continuing education courses, and enrollments had increased by an average of 10 percent annually for several years. He had asked several key staff members to prepare strategic plans for the division; his two most trusted colleagues had prepared reports with seemingly different assessments of what needed to be done. Now he had to decide which recommendations to follow. The issues with which he was grappling were, he knew intuitively, at the core of what Grant's institutional role should be in dealing with adult learners.

BACKGROUND

Grant University was founded in 1910, and has been an important part of the Detroit community since that time. It is comprised of five units: the College of Arts and Sciences, the College of Education, the School of Business, the Law School, and the Division of Continuing Education. Known locally as "the working man's school," Grant had catered to two population groups: the children of those in the emerging middle class, children whose parents wanted them to attend a private rather than public university, but who wanted (or needed) to live at home; and adults who were working full-time and financing their own education on a part-time basis. Indeed, for many years more than half of the FTEs for the university were part-time students, and a substantial majority of business students attended on a part-time basis.

Located near the center of the city's business district, Grant University was very much an urban institution, with no dormitories and with two converted office buildings as a campus. Recreational facilities were shared with the Detroit YMCA, which owned them. Because the university had a long tradition of part-time and evening study, its physical plant was well utilized during the week—classes were scheduled from 8:00 AM to 10:00 PM—but not effectively used on weekends.

Grant University is heavily dependent on tuition income, as it has been since its founding. Tuition dependency has forced Grant administrators to be market conscious, to be aggressive in developing new programs, and to terminate marginal programs. Faculty awareness of tuition dependency is manifested in the unusually strong advising program of the university.

THE DIVISION OF CONTINUING EDUCATION

The Division of Continuing Education (DCE) was established in 1976 to offer noncredit courses in the evening. Within a few years, DCE began offering courses during the day; it also assumed responsibility for offering the credit-based certification programs in education, nursing, and accounting. Because it did not offer degrees, the division was seen by some faculty as less pivotal to the university's mission. On the other hand, there were three achievements which had the cumulative effect of making DCE important to Grant:

- DCE provided additional income to faculty members
- DCE operated with an annual surplus, and thus contributed to the University's financial stability
- DCE served as a "magnet," drawing students to its courses many of whom later enrolled in degree programs

Beginning in 1983, the DCE began some outreach efforts. One involved lunchtime seminars offered on a noncredit basis. Any group of twelve or more individuals could sign up for short-term courses (the average length of each course was six sessions), and the instructor would come to the office for the sessions. Subsequent follow-up studies revealed that the lunchtime seminars were an important marketing device for Grant; nearly 40 percent of all newly enrolled degree students in the university had taken one or more courses through the continuing education division.

In 1995, DCE was authorized to award a bachelor of general studies (BGS) degree for students over thirty who had previously completed at least twenty-four college-level credits. This program intensified the efforts of DCE to concentrate on adult students. Four "adult counselors" worked with prospective students to review transcripts and to plan academic programs. Under the direction of Kimberly Scott, the coordinator of women's programs, a program for "reentry women" was created that offered up to forty credits at a discounted tuition. These efforts increased the number of students over twenty-five, and the median age of students in DCE increased by seven years from 1995 to 2000.

Developing an Effective Strategy to Increase Revenue: Recruiting or Retention?

Finances were a perennial issue for Edwards and all the other senior administrators at Grant. There was a long-standing commitment to keep tuition low, but there was also constant pressure to allocate funds for new program development, expanded services to students, and faculty development. Edwards was asked to develop a strategic plan for DCE that would double the net revenue over the next five years. The president had said: "I see some rough times ahead, and DCE is one of the few places where I think we can achieve revenue growth. I need your plan quickly, and I need it to work." Edwards immediately asked his two key deputies to develop recommendations about how DCE could achieve its mandate to increase net revenue for the university.

Associate Dean Neal Miller argued that "*our goal should be active recruiting.* DCE's appeal should be its low cost, its variety of offerings, and its convenience in terms of scheduling and location. While we have an interest in having DCE serve as a magnet to other Schools at Grant, our job is—and should be—service to the burgeoning population of people who want an organized, structured learning experience." He added, "Personally, I see nothing wrong with providing a 'revolving door' of opportunities for adult learners. Some will take a single course, some will take sources occasionally or regularly as their interests and needs change, and some will, indeed, become degree candidates at DCE or other schools at Grant. I think we should commit our energies and resources toward marketing like crazy!"

Kimberly Scott was DCE's director of Student Services. She was responsible for the counseling center, the placement office, and the learning center. Her approach was very different from Miller's: "Because we serve people who have in the past been outside the higher education mainstream, *we must make a concerted and visible effort to give them the support services necessary to help them remain enrolled,* and succeed in achieving their goals." She argued forcefully for her position, saying, "We have an obligation to pay attention to our students, as individuals, as learners, but most important, as individuals living in a complicated and demanding society. I disagree with Neal's 'revolving door.' I want to attract students to Grant, and retain them after they enroll."

Edwards thought wistfully of colleagues at other institutions where resources were not so tight, and where both strategies might be tried simultaneously. But he knew he had to make a choice, and he hoped that he would make the right one. . .

QUESTIONS FOR CONSIDERATION AND DISCUSSION

1. In what ways will recruiting more students help to alleviate Grant University's enrollment and financial challenges? What are the advantages to this approach? What are some possible drawbacks or limitations to this approach?
2. In what ways will retaining students and expanding services for them help to alleviate Grant University's enrollment and financial challenges? What are the advantages to this approach? What are some possible drawbacks or limitations to this approach?
3. How could the enrollment and financial challenges at Grant have been avoided or minimized? What would you have done differently in order to stave off declining enrollments?
4. What specific advice would you give Regan Edwards? What should be immediate actions, and what are longer-term considerations? How can Grant University evaluate the effectiveness of the recommendations you make?

PROFILE #14: ALDERSON STATE COLLEGE (INSTITUTIONAL ISSUES)

Rick Bedell was perplexed. He had been a member of the chancellor's staff as a budget analyst for nearly five months, and this was his first major assignment. He wanted to do a good job, and felt that he had the technical training and experience necessary. Still, he worried about whether he understood the chancellor's intentions, and whether in a brief position paper he would be able to analyze the issues clearly and succinctly.

A little more than a year before, the new chancellor had brought in a group of consultants to recommend a budgetary and accounting system for all the public higher education institutions in New Meridian. Their recommendation, which was adopted, was to use cost accounting to provide consistent and clear information to management. Quoting authoritative sources, their report said: "The process of cost accounting has developed because normal financial accounting procedures are totally inadequate for many managerial functions. Cost accounting is specifically designed to assist in decision making at all levels of management and produces reports at regular and timely intervals. Cost accounting is a management accounting system. Managers need cost information for a variety of reasons—evaluating, planning, pricing."

Bedell's assignment was to analyze the 2001–02 budget of the Division of Continuing Education at Alderson State College. Using conventionally accepted cost accounting procedures, Bedell had decided to divide his analysis into four areas:

- *Electing cost objects*
- *Assigning direct costs*
- *Assigning indirect costs*
- *Determining other principles and issues*

Beyond this, however, he knew that cost data provided "only half of the criteria necessary for informed judgment." He realized that he also needed to provide information regarding the organizational and social benefits. The crux of his dilemma was that the determination of social benefits in educational institutions was extremely difficult because they did not fit into a "monetary calculus." He was determined to make his financial analysis useful both in assessing educational endeavors and in controlling costs.

Background

Located in a suburb of Apex City, Alderson State College is one of the best-known public higher education institutions in the state. Apex City is the largest city in New Meridian, and industrial state in the Midwest. Alderson State, which began as a teacher-training school, developed bachelor's level programs in liberal arts, education and business after World War I, and began offering graduate programs in the 1950s. From its inception, Alderson State encouraged part-time study and continuing education; nearly half of its degree students studied on a part-time basis at some point, and its continuing education programs were popular, indeed, oversubscribed in some instances. And, while student enrollments in the "day credit" division had remained relatively stable for the past several years, student enrollments in continuing education had increased from approximately five thousand in 1995–96 to over seven thousand in 2001–02.

As a public institution, Alderson State receives most of its support from the state. The New Meridian Legislature approved a 2001–02 budget for Alderson State providing support of $140 per enrollment for *credit* courses in continuing education; noncredit courses generate no state revenue. Tuition prices, also established by the legislature, are as follows: credit courses, $60; noncredit courses, $30. Table 4.1 summarizes total income in continuing education.

The Division of Continuing Education

The Division of Continuing Education enjoys considerable flexibility in program planning and program logistics. For example, there are no restrictions on off-campus locations, and classes are held in

TABLE 4.1: Calculation of Total Income

Income Source	Evening Program	Off-Campus Program	Noncredit Program
Tuition income	4,000 enrollments @ $60 = $240,000	2,420 enrollments @ $60 = $145,200	960 enrollments @ $30 = $28,800
State revenue	4,000 enrollments @ $140 = $560,000	2,420 enrollments @ $140 = $338,000	
Total Income	**$800,000**	**$484,000**	**$28,800**

numerous places, rented commercially. Each year, the state auditor established a "negotiated overhead rate," reflecting the ratio of indirect to direct costs for each public institution. The overhead rate for Alderson State for 2001–02 is 55 percent of direct costs. Table 4.2 summarizes the Continuing Education Budget at Alderson State. There are three principal activities within the

Table 4.2:   Continuing Education Budget

Expense Category	Budgeted Amount ($)
Instructors:	
Evening program (part-time only, 185 courses)	190,000
Off-campus program (part-time only)	128,000
Noncredit program	27,000
Materials for noncredit program	1,000
Rent for off-campus program	28,000
Director of continuing education	31,000
Assistant director of continuing education	22,000
Director of off-campus programs	18,000
Administrative support	18,000
Fringe benefits	25,000
Promotional costs (all programs)	26,000
Special mailing for noncredit programs	5,000
Other costs (travel, telephone, etc.)	51,000
Total Budget	**$570,000**

Table 4.3:   Overview of Enrollments

Program	Courses	Enrollments	Participant Learning Hours (PLH)
Evening program	250	4,000	150,000
Off-campus program	110	2,420	90,750
Noncredit program	80	960	11,500
Totals	**440**	**7,380**	**252,250**

Division of Continuing Education, and a summary of the courses and enrollments of each program are detailed in Table 4.3.

The evening program offers its courses for part-time adult students. Only 185 of these courses are staffed by part-time instructors on the continuing education payroll; an additional sixty-five are staffed by part-time instructors on the continuing education payroll; as part of their load. Most of these full-time faculty members are in the College of Liberal Arts which, like many others, has "excess teaching capacity"; that is, the College of Liberal Arts has fewer students than it would need in order to have the faculty fully utilized.

The off-campus program is staffed entirely by part-time faculty; there is a full-time program director. Most of the course offerings are in business-related fields, and all courses are offered on a degree-credit basis. The off-campus programs pay $28,000 in rent for the various locations utilized.

The noncredit program also uses part-time instructors exclusively, and classes meet on campus. In general, noncredit courses meet for two hours weekly for six weeks. On the other hand, credit courses meet, on an average, three times per week for fifty-minute sessions over a fifteen-week period.

EFFORTS TO USE COST ACCOUNTING AT ALDERSON STATE

Bedell wanted his report to be clear and free of jargon. He decided to use some new terminology rather than relying on terms with possibly different connotations for some people, and used the following terms:

Level 1 costs are classroom costs. They include such resources as teachers or other learning facilitators, materials used by the learner, rented teaching equipment, or facilities.

Level 2 costs are incurred in planning and organizing the activity. They include costs for administrators, administrative support workers, curriculum development, supplies, or office occupancy directly associated with the administration of the program.

Level 3 costs are the general expenses of operating the organization. They include personnel costs that are not directly linked to any of the organization's programs, such as the executive offices or accounting services. They also include the cost of facilities for learning activities when these facilities are part of the organization plant and not paid for out of pocket. This means that classroom costs are included here when they cannot be broken out, even though by definition they belong in Level 1.

As he began his analysis, he started with determining *cost objects:* "an object may be a course, a set of courses, a program, a department, or any array of functions or activities." Rick believed this to be straightforward in the Division of Continuing Education, and he had the cost objects coincide with the three programs: evening, off-campus, and noncredit. Next, he divided costs into direct and indirect costs using a simple formula: "Costs that can be related easily and directly to a cost object are direct costs. All other costs are indirect costs." Table 4.3 illustrates Bedell's efforts in assigning costs.

Bedell then allocated the indirect costs using four principles:

1. The basis for assigning indirect costs should be reasonable and suggest a causal connection.
2. The basis should be consistent and quantifiable. It should not depend simply on management discretion regardless of the level of the understanding and good judgment.
3. The basis should be convenient and inexpensive to administer, and should rely on generally available data for determining allocation.
4. The basis should be understandable by the users of the information. If it is too complicated it will not be understood.

Tables 4.4 and 4.5 provide results and additional information on the assignment of both direct and indirect costs.

Having completed the technical aspects of the cost accounting analysis, Bedell was faced with the task of analyzing its significance, and raising policy issues which the chancellor and others would need to consider.

There were substantive financial issues to consider and resolve. For example, although the evening program operated at a surplus, it was clear that potentially greater surpluses are reduced by the very high cost of full-time faculty. If the College of Liberal Arts continues to "assign" people to teach in the evening program, what are the long-term implications in terms

Table 4.4: Assignment of Costs to Continuing Education Programs

Cost Category	Evening Program	Direct Costs Off-Campus Program	Noncredit Program	Total	Indirect Costs	Total Costs
Level I Costs						
Instructors:						
Part-time	$190,000	$128,000	$27,000	$345,000		$345,000
Full-time	160,000			160,000		160,000
Fringe	45,000			45,000		45,000
Materials			1,000	1,000		1,000
Rent		28,000		28,000		28,000
Level II Costs						
Director, continuing education					31,000	31,000
Assistant director, continuing education					22,000	22,000
Director, off-campus programs		18,000		18,000		18,000
Secretaries					18,000	18,000
Fringe benefits		5,000		5,000	20,000	25,000
Promotional			5,000	5,000	26,000	31,000
Other					51,000	51,000
Total Costs	**$395,000**	**$179,000**	**$33,000**	**$607,000**	**$168,000**	**$775,000**

of profitability? How could the institution's overall needs be meshed with specific interests in the Division of Continuing Education? Also, as Bedell looked at specific items in his analysis, he noted that difference in cost per participant and per PLH between the evening program and the off-campus program were related to differences in class size.

He speculated about how class size could be increased in the evening program. He also wondered whether it would be possible to reduce the very high cost per PLH in the noncredit program. As he examined the off-campus program further, he realized that it showed a considerable surplus, despite an excessively high overhead.

Bedell believed that, apart from issues of efficiency and cost effectiveness, there were two additional significant concerns: quality control and public service. Alderson State's "day-credit" programs enjoyed an excellent reputation throughout the state, and Bedell was aware that the Division of Continuing Education sought to maintain similar standards of excellence. A focal point for concern about quality was the off-campus program and the ability to maintain standards similar to that of the home campus. He also recognized that some noncredit offerings represent important public service initiatives. Thus, while the noncredit program operated at a considerable deficit, there were nonfinancial benefits, such as good will with particular constituencies.

Furthermore, there was some evidence to suggest that the noncredit program served as a "feeder" to credit programs. All of these issues needed to be analyzed and addressed in his report to the chancellor. As he reviewed the various budget information and worksheets (see Table 4.5; Worksheets 4.1 and 4.2), he quickly realized that it was a formidable task.

Questions for Consideration and Discussion

1. What are some of the direct costs associated with operating the programs at Alderson State College? What are some of the benefits associated with those costs, and who receives the benefits?

2. To what extent are quantitative measures, such as costs, important in determining the future directions of individual programs? How can leaders balance both quantitative and qualitative approaches to using information in decision making?

3. What specific advice would you give Rick Bedell, and why?

TABLE 4.5:   ASSIGNMENT OF INDIRECT COSTS TO CONTINUING EDUCATION PROGRAMS
AT ALDERSON STATE COLLEGE

	Evening Program	Off-Campus Program	Noncredit Program	Total Continuing Education
Direct costs	$395,000	$179,000	$33,000	$607,000
Indirect costs of continuing education division	95,000	42,000	31,000	168,000
Total Level 1+2 costs	490,000	221,000	64,000	775,000
Institutional overhead	269,000	122,000	34,000	425,000
Total costs	759,000	343,000	98,000	1,200,000
Total income	800,000	434,000	29,000	1,313,000
Surplus (deficit)	41,000	141,000	(69,000)	113,000
Total cost per course	3,036	3,118	1,225	2,727
Total cost per participant	190	142	102	163
Total cost per PLH	$5.06	$3.78	$8.52	$4.76

Worksheet 4.1: Steps in Budget Analysis

1. Examine continuing education budget (Table 4.2)

2. Compute income (See Table 4.1)

3. Assign direct costs (See Table 4.3)

   Note: Costs related easily and directly to **cost objects**[1]

4. Assign indirect costs (See Table 4.4)[2]

Note: Costs associated with the administration of continuing education.

5. Compute overhead (See footnote "c", Table 4.4)

   Note: Costs associated with overall operations of Alderson State College.

6. Calculate total cost (See Worksheet 4.2)

☐ by program
☐ by cost per participant
☐ by cost per PLH

7. Analyze financial and policy issues

[1] A **cost object** may be a course, a set of courses, a program, a department, or an array of functions or activities that can be assigned to a particular program.

[2] There are two basic rules to apply when establishing indirect costs: first, be reasonable and consistent; and second, make sure the rules are convenient, inexpensive to administer, and relatively easy to understand.

Worksheet 4.2: Calculating Total Costs of Programs

Including Direct, Indirect & Overhead Costs

Cost Category	Amount ($)
1. Add direct costs (Level 1)[1]	
2. Add indirect costs (Level 2)[2]	
Subtotal	
3. Multiply by established overhead (Level 3) @ 55%	
Total	

[1] See case study for definitions of cost levels.
[2] Use this procedure to determine indirect costs.

Allocate the indirect costs on the basis of **proportion** of total courses offered to calculate percent of total to be allocated to each cost object.

$$I = \%$$

Multiply total amount of indirect costs by percent to be allocated.

$$\$X \% = \$X$$

PROFILE #15: "THE CHOICE IS YOURS" (INSTITUTIONAL ISSUES)

Wayne Nethro sat in the provost's reception area, waiting for his appointment. The phone call from Provost Peter Fordyce had been unexpected and Nethro was mildly apprehensive about the meeting. He had speculated that the meeting was about a member of the English department faculty who was up for tenure; this is probably going to be bad news, he thought. Nethro's administrative assistant, Fran Hastings, thought the meeting was for another purpose. "The word on the street is that there are going to be more budget reductions," she said to Nethro, "and I think he'll tell you that we can't continue the search for the new tenure-track faculty member."

"Come in, come in," Fordyce said, warmly greeting Nethro. "It's rare these days to be able to sit down and talk with the chair of the college's largest department." After a few minutes of pleasantries, Nethro said: "Give it up, Pete. You're as nervous as a rookie pitcher. What's up, or should I say, how bad is the news?" Fordyce chuckled. "You know me too well, Wayne, and I'm sure Fran has her ear to the ground, as usual. How bad is the news? Well, it isn't good."

BACKGROUND

Nethro and Fordyce worked at Ravenal State College, one of eight colleges comprising the state college system. Ravenal was more than a century old, and had a statewide reputation for its excellent teacher education and nursing programs. Originally founded as a "normal school" to train teachers, Ravenal had become a comprehensive undergraduate college in the 1930s, and had begun offering selected master's degrees in the 1960s. Ravenal's largest academic department was the English department, with more than forty faculty members. The English department was responsible for the two-course sequence, Writing and Critical Thinking, required of all undergraduates, and a variety of literature courses used to satisfy the undergraduate general education requirement. In addition, virtually all the programs in the School of Education required undergraduate and graduate students to take literature courses.

In the early 1990s, when Nethro joined the English department, a faculty position in that department was considered

quite plum, with excellent job security, hard-working and qualified students, and strong programs recognized throughout the
state. Times changed, however, and gradually both the college
and the English department lost enrollments and luster. There
were numerous reasons for the decline. First, the state university
opened a branch campus in 1994 only fifteen miles from Ravenal's
campus. Originally established as a two-year branch, the state
university expanded to a four-year program in 1999. Second, at
approximately the same time, West Central State College, another
of the eight state colleges, began a distance learning master's program in secondary education, and within three years, graduate
enrollments at Ravenal had decreased by a third. English department enrollments were particularly hard hit because the largest
concentration in the secondary education master's program was
in English literature and writing. Third, high school students
throughout the state were taking advantage of advanced placement testing in order to waive some required courses in college;
the number of freshmen "waivers" increased from less than 10
percent in 1992 to nearly 40 percent a decade later.

The Enrollment Decline

Wayne Nethro became chairman of the English department in
2000. With forty-five full-time faculty members, and about thirty
adjuncts, the English department offered close to three hundred
courses each academic year, in several distinct categories (See
Table 4.6). Nethro and his faculty colleagues noted the decline
in course enrollments, but were not alarmed. An older member
of the department offered this assessment: "These are fads which
should not concern us. There will always be an English department here at Ravenal, and we should continue to do the things we
do well, and ride out the temporary popularity of West Central.
We're here to stay!"

The enrollment erosion continued, however, and by 2003,
Nethro only hired two adjuncts to teach in a very specialized area.
In fact, for the first time, he was having difficulty finding enough
courses for his full-time faculty to teach. Table 4.7 shows that there
were now forty-seven full-time faculty members in the following
categories.

Table 4.6: Course Offerings in the English Department (by Category)

Category	Courses
Required writing (two-course sequence)	80
General education requirements	35
Writing and literature electives	30
Courses to support education students (undergraduate)	60
Courses to support education students (graduate)	65
Service courses to other departments (graduate)	20
Other	10
Total	**300**

He could expect three or four retirements over the next several years, and one associate professor was rumored to be under consideration for a job at the state university. Two of the fourteen candidates for tenure would almost certainly not make it because of their generally unsatisfactory performance. Even if all of those people left, and he did not rehire the two temporary faculty, he would still have a faculty of thirty-eight. Looking carefully at enrollment trends, and the recent projections made by the Office of Enrollment Services, Nethro concluded that within two years, there would only need to be 200 courses offered each academic year. A faculty of thirty-eight, he knew, should be teaching about 230 courses each year.

He thought of several different strategies, and discreetly talked to colleagues and friends at other institutions. Some suggested that the English department embark on a recruiting campaign to attract more students; others suggested that the department

Table 4.7: English Department Faculty

Professors (with tenure)	13
Associate professors (with tenure)	15
Assistant professors (with tenure)	3
Associate professors (tenure track)	4
Assistant professors (tenure track)	10
Instructors and other temporary	2

develop some off-campus and continuing education programs; still others suggested that Nethro approach Provost Fordyce to see if the college could offer an early retirement incentive program that might reduce the faculty size by another three or four people. Nethro concluded that it would be difficult, if not impossible, to persuade his faculty colleagues that the problem was real, and that something had to be done. His faculty was appropriately proud of their success over the years, and of their statewide reputation for excellence. In the end, he decided that the best thing to do was to form a departmental committee to examine the recent enrollment decline, and make recommendations about next steps.

An Institutional Crisis

In the previous summer, the legislature mandated a 4 percent budget reduction each year for three years in all eight of the state colleges in order to deal with a budget deficit that was "out of control." Fordyce called a meeting of department chairs and other administrators, and announced a 10 percent reduction in supplies and equipment. He said that the possibility of faculty retrenchment was "very real," and he urged departments to be creative and aggressive in thinking about how to attract and retain students. In the meeting, he turned to Nethro and said, "Wayne, you head our largest department. If the English department can play a leadership role, it will be great for institutional morale." Nethro went back to the department, called a meeting, but, predictably, his faculty colleagues were reluctant to change the status quo. One faculty member even quoted Thoreau: "Never judge the climate of a region by a single cloudy day."

"Wayne," Fordyce began, "the time has come for making some tough decisions. You either need to find a substantial new market of students, or you need to reduce your faculty by approximately fifteen people. There is simply no other way to deal with this situation." "Peter," he said, "what can I do? Cutting the faculty would be devastating, and you know that. We would undoubtedly lose some of the bright young people we've hired in recent years, and be left with some of our least productive tenured faculty."

Fordyce said, "The chancellor has an idea. He thinks that we can market some off-campus programs from your department. He says there are dozens of companies that want to offer ESL programs, technical writing programs, and business writing programs on-site. He thinks we can get contracts to do that. He also thinks we can offer some continuing professional education programs for teachers, in the schools, on weekends." Nethro started to protest, but Fordyce raised his hands to silence him. "I want to meet with you next week. You should either bring a retrenchment plan, or a strategic plan about how to prepare for these new ventures. The choice is yours."

QUESTIONS FOR CONSIDERATION AND DISCUSSION

1. To what extent are the enrollment challenges confronting the English Department at Ravenal consistent with broader higher education trends and directions? What can disciplines with declining enrollments do in order to retrench and remain viable?
2. How can Wayne Nethro convince his faculty colleagues of the need for bold action? What specific recommendations might you make to him concerning "selling" this idea to his faculty?
3. In what ways might faculty be resistant or reluctant to new plans? In what ways, and by whom, might support for the new plan be manifested?
4. What are other strategies to contain costs and/or grow revenue for departments with limited enrollment? How might such a strategy be developed and implemented?

PROFILE #16: THE BOTTOM LINE (INSTITUTIONAL ISSUES)

"It isn't working, Pat, and you need to shut it down or make some big— and I mean really big—changes." Hal Needham closed his notebook, and looked directly at the president, whose face showed her concern and anxiety. As president of Maybank College, Pat Seger had worked tirelessly to return the college to a solid financial base and to develop new programs that reached beyond Maybank's traditional student constituencies. Now, if her business vice president was right, both goals were in jeopardy. The board meeting to consider the next year's budget was only two weeks away, and Seger knew that there would be the usual questions about controlling costs and avoiding a deficit. And, she thought apprehensively, the proposal to establish a weekend master's program was scheduled to be voted on. "Hal," she said, "I know we've been through this before, but is there any way to make this program cost-effective?"

Background

Maybank College celebrated its centennial in 1981 with a record of success and stability that was solidly respectable. Founded as a "ladies' academy" in a small prosperous community just outside Cleveland, it had been a popular choice for Cleveland families for decades. In the mid-1970s, however, the College began to face increased competition from the rapidly expanding state college system, and its traditional constituency eroded as more young women elected to attend colleges farther away, or chose to attend a coeducational institution. By 1980, Maybank's enrollments were only half of what they had been in 1965, and the college was in financial trouble for the first time. Between 1980 and 1993, Maybank had two presidents, one who was "an unmitigated disaster" and another who was "merely ineffectual." When Pat Seger became president in 1994, morale was low, enrollments uncertain, and finances precarious.

Seger was energetic and tenacious. She described herself to the presidential search committee as a "pragmatic idealist" who knew "you can only create beautiful dreams after you've paid the rent." She was effective and popular; some said it was the other way around, and that she was able to get things done *because* she was popular. She cut costs, traveled frequently to recruit students, and encouraged faculty and staff to propose and develop new programs.

Slowly, enrollments began to grow as new programs were proposed and implemented. Seger's strategy was to provide a small amount of seed money, to give program planners two or three years to demonstrate both programmatic success and cost-effectiveness, and encourage people to "work, work, work."

Two programs were illustrative of her approach. The first was the Friends of the Library project. The college's librarian, concerned about cuts in the budget for acquisitions, had organized the library staff, some faculty, and some area alums to have two or three discussion groups and readings each month. A small admission fee was charged, volunteers prepared refreshments, and library staff volunteered to coordinate the program. In 1999, the project contributed nearly $8,000 toward the purchase of new books. Hal Needham was unimpressed; "it costs us *something* to be running this, and I know that a lot of the work done by staff is done when they could be doing job related work. I doubt that it even breaks even." Seger said, "It's the sense of momentum that matters, and they feel that the money does make a difference."

The other project involved reaching out to the area's growing Latino population. Maybank offered several noncredit courses in English as a Foreign Language (EFL) on evenings and weekends. Classes were limited to fifteen students, who paid $100 for the twelve-week course. Faculty were paid a flat rate of $750. Seger was enthusiastic because she thought the program was helping a needy group, because it provided some extra money for faculty, and because the faculty involved were very enthusiastic about what they were doing.

When Needham gave her his financial analysis of the EFL program (see Exhibit 4.1), she said, "I'm sure you're right about all these indirect (and intangible) costs, but sometimes the financial bottom line isn't the only thing that matters."

EXHIBIT 4.1: NEEDHAM'S ANALYSIS OF THE EFL PROGRAM

Interoffice Memo
Pat,
Here is the fiscal analysis of the EFL program. We're losing money, and we need to raise tuition or cut faculty salaries (which is the biggest item in the budget).
Hal

Income	Amount	Total
83 students @ $100		**$ 8,300**
Expenses		
Faculty (6 @ $750)	$4,500	
FICA on faculty salaries	$344	
Mailings and brochures	$275	
Radio and newspaper ads	$350	
Books and supplies @ $6.25 *per student*	$519	
Extra security (12 Saturdays @ $65)	$780	
Clerical aides for registration	$170	
Subtotal	$6,938	
Indirect costs @ 29%	$2,012	
Total	**$8,950**	**$8,300**
Surplus (Loss)		**($650)**

QUESTIONS FOR CONSIDERATION AND DISCUSSION

1. To what extent does it make sense for an institution to offer an otherwise worthwhile program that may not be "profitable"? Under what conditions is this advisable?
2. Should Maybank College, or any institution, offer revenue-neutral or revenue-negative offerings? Why or why not? What is the "educational case" that can be made? What is the "business case" that can be made?
3. What issues and considerations must institutional leaders and faculty consider as they develop and implement programs? What evaluative criteria need to be identified and utilized, and how can a program's effectiveness be determined?
4. What specific advice do you have for Pat Seger? What challenges and opportunities might she face in adopting your advice?

PROFILE #17: A PROMISING PARTNERSHIP (INSTITUTIONAL ISSUES)

Tom Walsh, vice-president for Human Resources at Consolidated Information Systems (CIS), arrived in his office somewhat earlier than usual. Although the purpose of the meeting was to review the second year of operation of the collaboration between CIS and Miles Standish University's College of Liberal Studies (CLS), he wanted to be able to direct the conversation toward long-range planning issues. Walsh would be meeting with Polly Jenning, vice-dean at CLS, Alyce Mead, the program coordinator, and others from the university.

Walsh knew that the operations to date had been smoothly and effectively administered, and the program was too new and too small to be able to make any broad generalizations. He wanted to continue the collaboration. Indeed, the "press" was good within CIS and throughout the business community, and there were no "storm clouds" on the horizon. But, Walsh was future oriented, and he wanted to make certain that in the future there would be a solid evaluation, not merely enthusiasm and rhetoric, on which to base future decisions and commitments.

BACKGROUND

As vice dean of the College of Liberal Studies (CLS) at Miles Standish University, Polly Jenning was responsible for designing and implementing programs for CLS consistent with the university's overall mission. Over a period of years, she instituted several noncredit outreach courses, including one for senior citizens. She developed the idea for a university-employer collaboration after hearing various CLS students and potential students describe the financial barriers and burdens they encountered in trying to pursue postsecondary education. She knew that employer-provided tuition benefits were a common means by which working adults financed their studies. As she later described it: "I was seeing *some* students eligible for tuition reimbursement from their employers, but why weren't there many more? What was keeping them from coming?"

Jenning decided to take the initiative and contacted the Chamber of Commerce requesting information about the city's major employers. Jenning believed that Miles Standish's College of Liberal Studies was in a unique position to successfully implement a university-employer collaboration. The university had a prestigious history, and its sprawling campus was located a short distance from the city's business district. The University's College of Liberal Studies was established in 1984 "for students who wish to continue their education primarily in the evening on a full-time or part-time basis." Although CLS served nontraditional students of all ages, its primary focus is on working adults in the 25–45 age group.

Jennings focused her attention on a single corporation: CIS. With more than four thousand employees, CIS had worldwide operations in computer systems design, manufacture, and sales. The company offered an extensive tuition benefits package, and about 34 percent of its workforce had little or no college. Moreover, CIS had a long history of providing training and development programs for its employees. Bernard Gold, chairman and chief executive officer of CIS since 1995, was a strong believer in liberal education, and had written an op-ed piece in the *Wall Street Journal* stating "Education in the liberal arts plays an important role in developing managers. It provides a vital perspective on the interrelationship and growing complexity of business and society." Jenning wrote directly to Gold who responded enthusiastically, referring her to Tom Walsh, the company's vice president for Human Resources. Walsh was particularly supportive of the program's liberal arts focus. "A liberal arts degree develops critical skills and gives a better perspective on work," he said.

After a series of meetings between CIS administrators and Jenning in the spring of 2000, an agreement was reached: beginning in fall 2001, Miles Standish University would offer courses in the humanities, social sciences, and natural sciences *on-site* at CIS headquarters. Participants could earn either an associate or bachelor of arts degree.

The First Two Years

The agreement called for courses to be taught by Miles Standish faculty four days a week in classrooms at CIS's downtown headquarters. The academic calendar for the program consists of two fourteen-week semesters (fall and spring) and one twelve-week summer session. Several (four to six) courses per semester would be offered with each meeting one day per week. The program was designed so that an employee could earn a bachelor's degree in liberal arts in five and a half years.

CIS assumed costs for tuition, half of the program coordinator's salary, plus other miscellaneous administrative and support items (See Exhibit 4.2). Penn assumed costs for faculty salaries, the remaining half of the program coordinator's salary, and some miscellaneous administrative expenses. Instead of *reimbursing* student's for tuition, CIS paid the full tuition for each participant directly to the university; students paid only a $50 application fee and the cost of textbooks.

Exhibit 4.2: Miles Standish University/Consolidated Information Systems

Education Program
CIS Expenditures
Academic Year 2001–02
Fall, Spring, Summer Semesters

Tuition (75–125 Course Units per Semester)

Fall 2001	$37,540.00
Spring 2002	$34,490.00
Summer 2002	$21,900.00
Total tuition charges	**$93,930.00**

ADMINISTRATIVE AND OTHER SUPPORT COSTS

Coordinator's salary	$10,500.00
Benefits	$2,009.00
Communications (mailings, duplication, etc.)	$775.00
Faculty travel stipends (17 × $300)	$5,100.00
Curriculum development	$1,500.00
Tutorial support and special workshops	$3,100.00
Total administrative and other costs	$22,883.00
Total cost to CIS	**$16,813.00**

Budget note. Miles Standish University assumes the cost of faculty salaries, the remaining half of coordinator's salary, plus other miscellaneous administrative expenses.

The new program was publicized aggressively with slogans such as:

**WHY NOT COMMUTE TO COLLEGE BY ELEVATOR?
EARN A B.A. AT CIS**

CIS also informed employees about the program by enclosing information with every paycheck for eight weeks. In addition, a series of briefing sessions led by Jenning and Walsh were held to further publicize the program. Approximately eight hundred CIS employees attended meetings.

Two hundred and forty CIS employees applied for admission to the program for Fall, 2001. Each applicant was interviewed by Jenning or another CLS representative; all admissions decisions were made by the university. One hundred and one students were admitted. An additional forty-five employees were given a "deferred" status, and encouraged to attend a university-sponsored writing workshop; twenty of twenty-eight students who did so were admitted for the following semester. When classes actually began in the fall, eighty CIS employees enrolled in the program. A large majority of the students were administrative support employees; approximately 80 percent were women.

In May 2002, at the end of the program's first year of operation, Jenning hired Lucy Roth, an educational consultant, to conduct an evaluation of the collaboration. The evaluation indicated that, overall, both organizations were pleased with the program's initial year. CIS employees cited the possibility for career advancement and promotion and life enhancement as two major motivating factors for participating in the program. Although CIS officials had emphasized that there was no "guarantee" of career mobility for those who participated in the program, they also made it clear that enrollment in the program "wouldn't hurt" one's chances for promotion.

The second year proceeded with few changes from the first. Enrollments remained constant (see Table 4.8). Walsh was interested in a more detailed and comprehensive program evaluation; he hoped to identify possible correlations between participation in the program and job performance. During the initial two years of operation, courses had been offered in a variety of areas, taught by some of the university's most respected and effective faculty.

Looking Ahead

Walsh was generally optimistic about the future of the collaboration; he wrote to Gold that "the program positions the company as a leader in employee education and development." He knew

TABLE 4.8:   ENROLLMENTS, FALL 2001 TO SPRING 2003

Semester Student Entered Program	Fall 2001		Spring 2002		Summer 2002		Fall 2002		Spring 2003	
Fall 2001	78	100	54	75	37	41	39	48	39	48
Spring 2002			21	27	11	11	16	18	17	20
Summer 2002					2	2	1	1	1	1
Fall 2002							12	16	10	16
Spring 2003									4	4
Total	78	100	75	102	50	54	68	83	71	89

that it would be several years before there could be sufficient longitudinal data to measure the impact on individuals. He was impatient, however, to set in motion an evaluation procedure that could answer some of the larger policy issues that he knew needed to be addressed.

There was a pause in the discussion. As he had anticipated, the initial part of the meeting dealt with present operations and some "tinkering" with budgets and logistics. Now, Walsh was ready to shift the focus of the meeting. He began to speak. "Can we turn our attention to a discussion of the long-term implications of this collaboration and how we can evaluate the broader issues? I'd like us to examine some issues and questions I think we need to address, and to brainstorm the future of this partnership."

Questions for Consideration and Discussion

1. To what extent can the program be made more efficient, both financially and in terms of opportunities for students? How can CIS employees be integrated into the overall CLS program? How can CIS provide the full array of student services available to those who study on campus?
2. Do you feel that these organizations work well together? What problems, if any, are evident in this partnership? To what extent was the program's success dependent on the vitality and effectiveness of its administrator?
3. What are the advantages of collaboration between a university and employer? What are the advantages and disadvantages of a broader tuition benefit program? Can an employer offer both types of education programs simultaneously? With what consequences?
4. How can the long-term impact and effectiveness of this partnership be measured and evaluated? What stakeholder groups would need to be consulted? In what manner, and how often?

Summary

Each profile in this chapter is necessarily structured to be open-ended, thereby permitting readers to analyze, reflect on, and consider how they might address similar issues in their own institutional context. We can, however, identify some common themes in these profiles and provide a brief discussion of how to better understand and support adult learners. Some of the *institutional issues* include ensuring that the institution recognizes adult learners as a key stakeholder; allocating sufficient resources for adult learner programs and services; making necessary changes to be responsive to marketplace demands for learning; and partnering with outside organizations to extend institutional reach.

Serving multigenerational learners in a resource-constrained environment is essentially the focus of *Bait and Switch*, in which tough choices and priorities have to be made concerning when and how to schedule courses for students. Cascade Valley State College marketed itself to adult learners as a setting in which their needs—including scheduling-related ones—would be accommodated. This represents a situation where what was promised initially to learners has not, for however worthwhile and valid reasons, been able to be sufficiently fulfilled. This also highlights the challenges of catering to learners with divergent needs, in this case students who need to attend classes both during the day and evening. One suggestion for administrators and faculty at Cascade Valley would be to determine the extent to which the institution is truly committed to adult learners. From there, aligning resources and priorities to support their needs must occur. In this particular scheduling situation, leveraging course management systems, online learning, or hybrid models, among other alternatives, might be an initial intervention worth pursuing.

The challenge of generating and allocating scare resources is also evident in the profile of Grant University, which is experiencing financial difficulty. This case reflects a challenge to spend money on either recruiting or retaining students, or both. Simply throwing additional dollars toward recruitment efforts—without properly having the services, structures, and support mechanisms in place to retain and graduate students—is foolish. Thus, Grant University administrators should consider several strategies. First, they should analyze the causes of student departure, identifying those issues that are personal, situational, or institutional, and attempting to remedy institution-oriented problems. Second, ensuring that the bottlenecks and pathways to persistence and graduation are cleared can be a helpful strategy in retaining students. Once internal issues of student retention are addressed, then attention can be turned to analyzing the effectiveness of recruitment practices, with particular attention to those strategies that yield the greatest return.

Analyzing student pathways into an institution is also the focus of Alderson State College's profile. Student enrollment patterns through a mix of credit, noncredit, on-campus, and community-based courses are reflective of the various instructional and programmatic approaches used at many institutions. Alderson State should conduct a cost-benefit analysis of offering its noncredit courses, in particular, and should ensure that its noncredit continuing education offerings produce fiscal self-sufficiency for the unit. One way to accomplish this is to assess community and corporate needs, and to analyze the extent to which noncredit offerings are truly the "feeder" into credit programs that Alderson State assumes. Like Cascade Valley and Grant University, Alderson State needs to sharpen its focus and prioritize its offerings based on documented demand and programs that students and other stakeholders value and are willing to pay for.

Being mindful of market-driven forces affecting colleges and universities, and being responsive to those forces, is further exemplified in both *The Choice Is Yours* and *The Bottom Line*. Each profile could easily be renamed *Innovate or Vacate*, as enrollment declines are potentially threatening the institution to initiate a reduction in force among its faculty ranks. Administrators at both Ravenal State and Maybank College must work with faculty, especially in the fiscally underperforming departments, to assist them in developing alternative courses in off-site and corporate settings. Faculty, too, owe their own individual and collective destinies to their ability to change and adapt to new educational realities.

The challenge, of course, is in preserving the longstanding and time-honored traditions of a particular discipline while contemporizing and expanding its appeal in settings beyond narrowly defined interests. Consulting colleagues in departments, either on campus or elsewhere, that have undergone revitalization is one suggestion. Also, actively assessing the needs of community and corporate partners, and translating those needs into solutions that the department or discipline can provide, is a way of expanding interest and appeal to others.

A Promising Partnership focuses on the types of partnerships that institutions can undertake to enhance their own revenue streams while simultaneously expanding educational opportunities to adult learners in settings beyond the ivory tower of higher education. This profile provides vivid details on the many different stakeholder needs, competing and complementary missions, and the complexities of launching and sustaining such initiatives. Of particular importance in this profile is an emphasis on evaluating the impact and effectiveness of such partnerships. Inherent in such an evaluation is the need to establish clearly defined goals and objectives at the outset, along with measures or performance indicators that are objective and based on evidence. Because of the many internal and external stakeholders who have a vested interest in partnerships such as the one profiled, it is necessary to proactively and continuously determine mechanisms to assess and evaluate quality and to make ongoing enhancements and improvements.

The *institutional issues* presented in these profiles are representative of just a few of the many possibilities and eventualities in supporting adult learners. Please refer to the Action Planning and Readings and Resources sections that follow to help you and enhance understanding of these issues in your own institutional context.

ACTION PLANNING

- Based on information presented in the preceding profiles, what are similar *institutional* issues related to adult learners at your college or university?
- What is your college or university doing especially well to understand and support *institutional* issues related to adult learners?
- In ways can your college or university improve its efforts to understand and support *institutional* issues related to adult learners?
- Where might support for improvement efforts be garnered? To what extent will there be any resistance to such efforts?
- What are immediate next steps? What are longer-term considerations?
- Other resources, suggestions, or ideas?

Readings and Resources

The following readings and resources are provided to expand knowledge on a particular *institutional issue* related to adult learners in higher education. Each was selected because it expands on a concept, idea, or approach highlighted in one or more profiles. A more comprehensive bibliography is included at the conclusion of this book.

Alexander, F. K., and Ehrenberg, R. G. (Eds.). Maximizing resources: Universities, public policy, and revenue production. *New Directions for Institutional Research, 119.* San Francisco: Jossey-Bass, 2003.

Astin, A. W., Keup, J. R., and Lindholm, J. A. A decade of changes in undergraduate education: A national study of system "transformation." *Review of Higher Education, 25*(2), 141–162, 2002.

Bueschel, A. C., and Venezia, A. (Eds.). Policies and practices to improve student preparation and success. *New Directions for Community Colleges, 145.* San Francisco: Jossey-Bass, 2009.

Burge, E. J. (Ed.). The strategic use of learning technologies. *New Directions for Adult and Continuing Education, 88.* San Francisco: Jossey-Bass, 2001.

Caffarella, R. S. *Planning programs for adult learners: A practical guide for educators, trainers, and staff developers.* San Francisco: Jossey-Bass, 2001.

Coomes, M. D., and DeBard, R. (Eds.). Serving the millennial generation. *New Directions for Student Services, 106.* San Francisco: Jossey-Bass, 2004.

Flint, T. A., Zakos, P., and Frey, R. *Best practices in adult learning: A self-evaluation workbook for colleges and universities.* Dubuque, IA: Kendall/Hunt, 2002.

Junco, R., and Timm, D. M. (Eds.). Using emerging technologies to enhance student engagement. *New Directions for Student Services, 124.* San Francisco: Jossey- Bass, 2009.

Kasworm, C. E. From the adult student's perspective: Accelerated degree programs. *New Directions for Adult and Continuing Education, 97,* 17–27, 2003.

Keeton, M., Sheckley, B., and Griggs, J. *Effectiveness and efficiency in higher education for adults: A guide for fostering learning.* Dubuque, IA: Kendall/Hunt, 2002.

Laanan, F. S. (Ed.). Understanding students in transition: Trends and issues. *New Directions for Student Services, 114.* San Francisco: Jossey-Bass, 2006.

Pappas, J., and Jerman, J. (Eds.). Developing and delivering adult degree programs. *New Directions for Adult and Continuing Education, 103.* San Francisco: Jossey-Bass, 2004.

Rice, P. J. Adult student service office. *New Directions for Student Services, 102,* 53–57, 2003.

Spangler, M. S. (Ed.). Developing successful partnerships with business and the community. *New Directions for Community Colleges, 119.* San Francisco: Jossey-Bass, 2002.

Tagg, J. *The learning paradigm college.* Bolton, MA: Anker, 2003.

Tinto, V. *Leaving college: Rethinking the causes and cures of student attrition* (2nd ed.). Chicago: University of Chicago Press, 1994.

Townsend, B. K., and Dougherty, K. J. (Eds.). Community college missions in the 21st century. *New Directions for Community Colleges, 136.* San Francisco: Jossey-Bass, 2007.

Wlodkowski, R. J., and Kasworm, C. E. (Eds.). Accelerated learning for adults: The promise and practice of intensive educational formats. *New Directions for Adult and Continuing Education, 97.* San Francisco: Jossey-Bass, 2003.

Wolf, M. A. (Ed.). Adulthood: New terrain. *New Directions for Adult and Continuing Education, 108.* San Francisco: Jossey-Bass, 2006.

CHAPTER FIVE

PROFILES OF POLICY ISSUES RELATED TO ADULT LEARNERS

The profiles in this chapter cover a variety of *policy issues* surrounding adult learners in higher education.

The Weakest Link profiles Wessex University, which has developed satellite locations that have helped raise enrollment. However, in recent years enrollment fluctuations have forced satellite directors to find a way to increase enrollment or cut back staff. It took a lot of work on Meredith's part to get the school to give the satellite directors greater autonomy, and Andy McVeigh is potentially taking advantage of his power. Recent decisions have cause Meredith to question his behavior, and she is orchestrating a meeting with her boss to discuss the situation, hoping to be able to come to a conclusion.

Coastal Military Installation (CMI) needed a better system for educating their personnel. Many people have postsecondary education, and Johnson feels that the best choice for now is to develop a master's program to continue the education of these individuals. He feels that this credential will allow them to function in that field that is more in line with their interests. After developing a committee of personnel to aid him, Johnson contacts local universities to decide which institution to hire to fulfill their needs—notably, CMI needs a school that is of reasonable cost, is willing to work with the credit that most students have, and is reasonable in their transfer credit policies. The committee has received proposals provided by the universities, and they now have to choose which provider will offer a master's degree to CMI students.

In *How Much Access Is Too Much Access*, North Meridian State University must evaluate its ACCESS program and figure out how to reduce its costs while still providing the accessibility the governor wants. The ACCESS program was created to provide an opportunity for those people over thirty but having no higher credentials than a high school diploma. It was funded using money from the state lottery. McPherson-Foote must figure out how to keep the program running while appeasing legislators who feel that it is wasting money.

The Base of the Pyramid deals with the necessity of more remedial courses at New Dorset Community College, which lacks funding from the state to implement the courses. Students are coming to college unprepared to do college-level work and if they are to succeed they must have remedial courses. Conterra must determine how to make the legislators understand this.

Finally, *How to Achieve an Appropriate Balance* focuses on the changing climate at Urban State University and Medical Center (USUMC). The campus is placing more emphasis on research at a time when new market entrants are competing for the institution's long-standing stakeholder: adult learners. Feng has developed a strategy that delivers a particular baccalaureate degree program entirely online, one that relies disproportionately on adjunct instructors. Leah needs to determine the faculty development strategy that can support such an approach.

PROFILE #18: THE WEAKEST LINK (POLICY ISSUES)

"Frank, it's Meredith. Listen, could I get on your calendar tomorrow for about forty-five minutes? I have some issues I want to talk to you about concerning the satellite centers." Meredith Blason-Tabor waited as she heard her colleague and boss, Frank Lombard, shuffle papers as he looked for his day planner. After listening to his response, she said, "No, it's not urgent. I've been thinking about how best to deal with enrollment shortfalls at the three satellites, and whether we need to make some adjustments to get the job done. OK. See you then."

Once off the phone, she thought, that was just the right tone—not too urgent, but serious. Now, all I have to do is figure out what to say when I meet with him tomorrow.

BACKGROUND

Wessex University was founded in 1914 to celebrate the two hundredth anniversary of the establishment of New Wessex Colony by British settlers eager to seek their fortunes and begin new lives in the New World. By the time the university was founded, the city of New Wessex was a thriving metropolis, an important commercial and financial center, the operating center for several of the largest commodity organizations in the country, and the fourth busiest port in the United States.

Wessex was organized as a private institution, although it received some subsidies from the city and state. The state's land grant institution was only twenty-five miles away and, in close proximity to WU, there were four other private institutions, two community colleges, and several for-profit proprietary schools. Although some of the universities were more highly regarded than others in particular areas, especially in graduate and professional fields, the market was highly competitive for undergraduate students.

Beginning in the 1970s, virtually all the universities in the area sought to create a market niche that would appeal to older, part-time students. Wessex, for example, developed a series of satellite campuses offering graduate programs within seventy-five miles of the main campus. Beginning with two satellites in 1979, by 2000 there were eleven satellites serving twelve hundred graduate students.

THE SATELLITE CAMPUS NETWORK

Initially, each satellite was organized to provide some—but not all—of the required courses to earn a degree. Typically, students could take required courses at a satellite, and then complete advanced courses on the main campus. For almost fifteen years, the university insisted that, for reasons of quality control, only full-time faculty members on the main campus could teach courses at the satellites. This, it was believed, would maintain consistency and quality. This proved to be impractical as the number of satellites grew, and in 1993 a decision was made to permit the SCD (Satellite Center Director) to hire part-time faculty to teach, with the stipulation that the faculty hired must use the university-approved syllabi for required courses. Part-time faculty teaching advanced courses were appointed by the SCD in conjunction with the appropriate academic dean on the main campus.

A REQUEST FOR GREATER AUTONOMY

By 1998, however, graduate enrollments in some programs had increased to the point where SDDs argued that they needed greater autonomy in academic areas. This was particularly true in three programs: the M.B.A., the M.S. in Information Technology, and the M.A. in Communication. There was at least one program at five of the eleven satellites; four of the satellites had two of the programs; and, two of the satellites had all three programs. The SDDs responsible for these programs requested authority in the following areas: approval of transfer credits and credit for prior learning for degree students; appointment of part-time faculty for advanced courses and seminars without approval from the main campus; making multiyear commitments to part-time faculty; and approval of student requests for independent study, internships, and online courses.

Wessex's vice president for Academic Affairs, R. Franklin Lombard, was reluctant to approve the request, which he felt would decentralize academic decision making, and leave the university vulnerable to criticism if student performance declined at a particular satellite. Lombard's associate vice president for Satellite Programs, Meredith Blason-Tabor, was a strong advocate for permitting SDDs to have more autonomy. She believed in decentralization and thought that the individual directors were in the best position to know what to do—and what was needed—for program success. Having oversight responsibility without having to be involved in operating decisions freed her time to work on academic planning and evaluation, her primary interests.

Furthermore, directors were appointed for three-year renewable terms, and there was a comprehensive evaluation submitted to Lombard before he made the decision of reappointment. Blason Tabor, who had developed the SPD evaluation system, and to whom the SPDs reported, believed they were all competent and responsible. Half of them had been faculty members at Wessex, and several others had taught elsewhere. Lombard had worked closely with Blason-Tabor when they were both academic deans at Wessex, and he respected her judgment.

In a meeting with Lombard, Blason-Tabor said, "Look. This is a franchise operation, and we need to have one person answerable for everything that goes on at each satellite. If something goes wrong, I want to be able to go to one person—only one person—and say, 'what happened?'" He accepted her plan, but he was clearly nervous, and said, "Watch this carefully." She believed this was a great opportunity both for her and for the SDDs to demonstrate leadership skills. By enabling the SPDs to exercise a great deal of autonomy in academic matters, Blason-Tabor knew she was substituting *review* for *engagement*, but she felt that if the SPDs had overall responsibility for balancing budgets, running overall operations effectively, they should also have authority to make decisions about academic programs and standards.

For two years, the "franchise" model appeared to work well. There were relatively few "infrastructure" problems between the satellites and main campus functions such as the registrar's office, the university library, the financial aid office, and several others. In fact, the report of the most recent reaccreditation visit to Wessex in 2000 had noted, "There is a clear and commendable division of responsibility between campuswide administrators and the directors of satellite program. The directors have considerable discretion in making academic and operational decisions. While this could be a problem in some circumstances, we believe that the oversight structure currently in place is an adequate 'safety net.' At the same time, we note that the management structure of the satellites is highly dependent on the competence and judgment of the directors."

ENROLLMENT DECLINES

After the events of 9/11/2001, overall graduate enrollments at the satellites declined almost 10 percent in two years, both as a result of a weaker economy and uncertain job prospects. The enrollment declines were concentrated in five satellites, whereas the remaining six continued to meet their graduate enrollment targets.

Three of the satellites, however, had serious enrollment short-falls. Blason-Tabor, with Lombard's approval, informed each of the SPDs that they would have to meet enrollment goals within twenty-four months. "The alternative to stopping enrollment shortfalls," she said, "would not be pleasant for you or for the satellite operations."

Andrew McVeigh, LeMoyne Washington, and Maryellen Durkin, the three affected SPDs, asked to meet with Blason-Tabor to discuss the future of their programs. McVeigh's satellite center had two graduate programs (in business administration and communication) and enrollment losses in both programs were in excess of 20 percent. Durkin's satellite center was the newest one in the Wessex network, and she had expected to have several years to build the programs at her center.

They argued that the present situation was a "blip," and that supplements to the marketing budgets of the satellites could "fix the problem." Blason-Tabor agreed that additional marketing would help, but she did not give them additional resources. Instead, she told them they could reallocate funds within their budgets, and, if necessary, make program and course "adjustments" to achieve greater cost-effectiveness, hire part-time faculty who would accept lower payment for their teaching, or "use any creative ideas you come up with" to meet enrollment goals. She asked each of them to develop a plan for her review.

Blason-Tabor believed that the coming months would be a test of the decentralized management system at Wessex. There had not been a financial situation as serious as this since the satellites had been opened, and if enrollments did not grow it would call into question *both* the managerial and leadership abilities of the SPDs, *and* the decentralized system she had helped develop and had vigorously supported. She knew the three SPDs had performed well in the past, but they had never worked under this kind of pressure, and she didn't know whether they would rise to the occasion, or falter as pressures increased.

SOME DISTURBING DEVELOPMENTS

A month later, Blason-Tabor received a copy of a letter the university registrar had written to McVeigh. The letter stated that four newly enrolled students had not taken the mathematics and

English proficiency placement exams required of all new students. Unless they took and passed the two exams, they could not enroll in subsequent semesters. She immediately called McVeigh, who told her that he had permitted them to register without taking the exams because "time was short." He continued, "I was rushing to get them enrolled so they could start this semester." She responded, "Let's avoid this kind of mess in the future." She thought this was a "kind of sloppy oversight," but let the matter drop.

At the beginning of the following semester, Blason-Tabor was holding a routine meeting with one of the program coordinators who reported to her to review petitions from satellite directors for exceptions to academic requirements. The program coordinator said that McVeigh had requested approval to accept thirty-nine transfer credits, but would not approve such an exception because they were rarely approved on the main campus, and it was not a good precedent. Within a day, McVeigh called to ask her to reconsider her decision. He was upset, but controlled, and Blason-Tabor could hear the tension in his voice. "This will be a disaster," he said, "because those students will not enroll unless we accept the thirty-nine credits, and if they don't enroll I will have to cancel two courses because of insufficient enrollments."

"Look, Andy," she said, "I would rather have us cancel a course than make exceptions to sound academic policy." McVeigh pressed his argument, but she would not yield. Finally, he said, "It's tough to meet 'enrollment targets' if you don't have the power to approve exceptions." She responded, "No one ever said that you should go for enrollments at the expense of academic standards." He retorted, "Don't you think we got the message when you said 'increase enrollments, or else'?" "You got a message," she said coldly, "but I'm not sure it's the one we wanted you to hear."

Blason-Tabor was troubled by these incidents, but she believed in the decentralized management model, and thought that McVeigh was probably feeling pressure and was jittery. She didn't like the potential erosion of academic standards, but decided to give the situation—and McVeigh—a chance to settle down.

A few weeks later, Frank Lombard and Blason-Tabor were walking across campus to a meeting, and he was filling her in on a lunch meeting he had with the dean of the School of Business to discuss pending curricular changes about to be presented. Almost as an afterthought, he said, "Meredith, do you remember that adjunct faculty member in business, Barney something or other?" Meredith laughed: "You mean Professor No Show?" "Well," Frank said, changing his tone so it was obvious that they were now at the level of gossip, not "official" business, "Walter [the dean of the school of business] said that Andy McVeigh hired him to teach two courses in spite of that mess last year, and that, guess what, he missed two classes in two weeks? So much for giving a guy a second chance." Blason-Tabor smiled, as if seeing humor in Frank's story, but she was furious.

At a meeting with SPDs the previous semester, she had recounted the problems on the main campus with that faculty member and she said, "I know some of you worry when you don't have adjunct faculty to cover your classes just before the start of the semester, but let's not ask for trouble. Steer clear of this guy." Now she was hearing for the first time that McVeigh had actually hired him, despite her warning.

CAUGHT BETWEEN PRINCIPLE AND PRAGMATISM

McVeigh was instantly defensive when he heard from Blason-Tabor. "First of all, I have the authority to hire part-time faculty, and I decided not to follow your 'suggestion.' I hired him because I needed him, and I think I made the right decision under the circumstances. Second, I don't have time to ponder every decision, and that's because of the pressure you are putting on me to increase enrollments." "Now look," she said, fighting to keep her voice steady, "your autonomy is based on satisfactory performance. You don't have the autonomy to do a bad job."

"You just said what some of us have thought for a long time. Your idea of decentralization is having us do what you want. I want to run a program, not simply implement it. Sure, I've been busy, and, sure, I've made mistakes, but I was hired to run this place, and that was fine with you until there was a problem. Now, please, step back, and let me do my job."

Blason-Tabor was troubled and conflicted by their exchange. She had always thought that McVeigh was competent, if not outstanding, and there had been few problems in the past.

She knew from past experiences that some managers buckled under pressure, and that might be what was happening here. What was obvious, however, was that McVeigh had become a weak link in the chain of SPDs, and that weakness could damage the Wessex satellite system, a system she had helped to build. If that occurred, her own reputation might be affected, and possibly her future opportunities as well. McVeigh was scheduled to be evaluated next year, and some of these problems would definitely surface then She could maintain things as they were, but it was very likely that the problems at the satellite would increase, and the overall situation could get worse. She could supervise him more carefully, but he would resent and resist that. Getting rid of him would call attention to his deficiencies, and could cause people to wonder if the decentralized model was working effectively. There didn't seem to be any good choices.

She pondered the situation and reviewed her options repeatedly. It was clear that she had to say something to Frank, her boss. They had worked together for a long time, and she knew that when she explained the situation he would say, "Well, Meredith, what are your options, and what do you want to do?"

She sat at her desk thinking about McVeigh's same blunders and seeming inability to operate effectively under pressure. She believed in decentralization, and wondered if one weak link could damage a fundamentally sound structure. Looking at the clock on the wall, she thought to herself, OK. You've got about twenty hours to figure this one out.

QUESTIONS FOR CONSIDERATION AND DISCUSSION

1. What are Meredith Blason-Tabor's concerns, and why are they important? What are Andy McVeigh's concerns, and why are they important? To what extent are each party's concerns convergent or divergent?
2. How can institutions which operate both "main" and "satellite" campuses balance the need for standardization and centralization against that of flexibility and decentralization? What are the strengths and challenges of each approach?
3. What advice would you give to satellite campus directors? What are the immediate concerns, and what are the longer-term challenges?

4. What are the central issues confronting academic programs offered by the same institution, but delivered in different venues or formats (such as classroom-based versus online)? How can administrators and faculty work together to overcome obstacles to differentiated approaches?

Profile #19: Coastal Military Installation (Policy Issues)

In reality, the educational program at Coastal Military Installation consisted of a cluster of courses in English, sociology, and psychology offered by a nearby community college. There were no systematic advising or program planning activities available. The two-person staff devoted itself mainly to paperwork, clearing personnel to attend classes off base, and preparing military transcripts of work completed for those leaving military service.

Coastal had survived the latest round of base closings and, in fact, had grown slightly as personnel from two nearby bases that were to be closed had been transferred to Coastal. But a 1999 Internal Review and Operational Audit had been critical of the educational program, describing it as "ineffectual" and "without focus." The colonel responsible for education programs at the command level had been ordered to make "substantial changes to increase the educational capabilities at Coastal." In due course, he appointed Ronald Johnson in 2001 as the base's Educational Services Officer (ESO) with a mandate to develop a degree-granting postsecondary educational program.

Background

Coastal Military Installation (CMI), situated twenty miles outside the capital of New Columbia, is a research, development, and procurement base with approximately four thousand personnel. Coastal has a national reputation for its research innovations in the military uses of electronics and radar. CMI is also the regional center for purchasing and procurement for the armed services, with purchasing responsibility for sixteen bases in a five-state area.

Johnson, a retired lieutenant colonel who had been hired as a civilian, was an experienced manager and educator. He had spent a tour of duty as a faculty member at the Army War College, had worked in the Pentagon's Office of Educational Programs and

Services, and had a reputation as a "fix it" manager. An old friend at the Pentagon who was familiar with the problems at Coastal wrote:

> Nothing has worked at Coastal, Ron. Things have been tried but they have failed. As you know, we aren't always able to give education the priority that we'd like to in this command, but we care about it. Our goals are recruitment and retention. We want someone to go into Coastal and get something going. It won't be easy.

Shortly after his arrival, Johnson set out to determine Coastal's educational needs, and began by examining the educational backgrounds of CMI's personnel, as shown in Table 5.1.

When he examined the fields of study of B.S. recipients, Johnson found academic concentrations clustered in three areas:

Academic Concentration	Number
Business administration and management	307
Engineering	270
Mathematics, and physical and natural sciences	49

TABLE 5.1: EDUCATIONAL LEVEL OF CMI PERSONNEL

Educational Level	
High school diploma	1,592
Some work beyond high school (including associate's degrees)	415
B.A./B.S	761
Some work beyond the B.A./B.S.	249
Master's	604
Some work beyond the master's	85
Doctorate (or equivalent terminal degree)	103
Total	**3,809**

The remaining 135 bachelor's recipients had studied in other areas, largely in education and the social sciences.

Another of Johnson's early tasks was a review of job descriptions and the educational qualifications of the personnel in those positions. He was surprised and dismayed at what he found. There were electrical engineers in management positions, technical personnel working as statisticians, and personnel with engineering and scientific backgrounds in procurement and purchasing. The developing picture revealed an installation with strong needs in engineering management, systems management, and accounting, purchasing, and procurement. As Johnson summed it up in a memorandum to the base commander, "We need graduate programs in business administration and engineering."

Although he was aware that there were pressing needs for undergraduate programs, Johnson decided that the greatest likelihood of success would be in the development of a master's level program. He knew that there were some excellent colleges and universities within a hundred miles of Coastal, and he decided to send a request for proposals to potential educational providers. Relying on the information he had, Johnson wrote a description of Coastal's requirements for a graduate program in management and engineering; this was distributed to all institutions in New Columbia, and some selected out-of-state schools.

Developing a Master's Program for CMI

To assist him in the decision-making process, Johnson created an advisory committee. He chose the chief engineer at CMI, the director of the largest research program currently under way, the chief of another base project who was a systems management graduate of a military school, a local ROTC commander, and the associate director of procurement, a career officer who had an MBA and more than twenty years of experience. Johnson would make the final decision, but would take the advisory committee's recommendation very seriously.

A few institutions, including some of the most well known and prestigious ones, did not reply. In all, the committee received fourteen responses. A few could be eliminated quickly; they offered proposals which appeared opportunistic, promising a suspiciously quick and easy route to a degree. Johnson was aware that critics contended that hucksterism was rampant in institutions offering such programs, but he—and the committee— were impressed at how many solidly conceived proposals were received.

Of the eleven remaining proposals, the advisory committee eliminated six for one or more of the following reasons:

- Transfer policies (credit given for courses taken elsewhere) were too stringent.
- Program requirements would result in an unreasonably lengthy time to degree completion.
- Resources were insufficient to deliver a strong program in management and engineering.
- Requirements for minimum class size were too high.

Invitations were then sent to five institutions (see Exhibit 5.1) to visit CMI, and make presentations to Johnson and the members of the advisory committee. Johnson asked the advisory committee to "recommend the institution which gives us the best combination of reputation, flexibility, and cost." In his written instruction to the advisory committee, he said:

Cost, naturally, is a major factor, particularly for the service, because the military normally pays the majority of tuition costs. I also believe that flexibility and responsiveness in the curriculum is crucial, as is the institution's reputation because we want the degree to be recognized as one of quality. Keep in mind, also, that prior experience in working with a military installation may be very important. Finally, we need an institution with a liberal policy of accepting transfer credit because a significant segment of the base population moved each year.

Johnson paused before entering the room. He had been told that the advisory committee had decided which institution to recommend, and wanted to meet with him, both to tell him of their decision, and to answer

any questions he might have. He had received a call from the base com-
mander the day before asking him when a final decision would be made.
He knew that the time for making a decision was at hand, and he hoped
that he would agree with, and could support, the recommendation from the
advisory committee.

EXHIBIT 5.1: PROFILE OF THE INSTITUTIONS SUBMITTING
PROPOSALS

Brownlow College was an out-of-state college with a strong national reputation. It had experienced considerable success with its distance programs, administered from the central campus, and it had programs on several military installations. Johnson was attracted to this dimension of experience. It meant that Brownlow brought a seasoned perspective to the problems of military education. On the other hand, Brownlow representatives revealed an inflexible approach to curriculum. They were confident of their rationales, and they expected to implement their own curriculum without alteration. For example, the suggestion that engineers learn to read an electrical schematic in an introductory course was rejected in favor of the general-preparation philosophy that Brownlow favored. Brownlow had a restrictive transfer policy: it accepted no transfer credits. The tuition would be $240 per semester hour.

Flagship State University would bring to Coastal the authority and facilities of the central campus of the state system. The resources of Flagship were the richest of the presenting institutions, and Flagship was prepared to be responsive and flexible in the curriculum, developing a program suited to base needs. The distance of the university campus from Coastal—a two-hour drive—presumably would not be a factor because Flagship proposed to implement its curriculum through extensive use of distance learning technologies. Several members of the board, applauding the use of technology in education, regarded this feature as a strength of the Flagship proposal. Johnson tended to prefer live faculty in the classroom. Flagship would accept six to nine hours of transfer credit from other institutions. As the state university, they were obliged to offer base students the state resident tuition rate, $140 per semester hour.

Hammond Bay College impressed the committee with a responsive and flexible approach to Coastal's needs. Although Hammond Bay was only an hour away, it would place its own assistant dean on the installation and give him absolute authority over curriculum, with emphasis on responding to direction from Coastal. Johnson saw Hammond Bay as providing an opportunity to develop a master's program uniquely suited to his population and also offering a basis for quality control. On the other hand, Hammond Bay was the smallest and least well known of all the institutions making presentations. Several committee members had never heard of it before, and they questioned the worth of a degree from a college that (though fully licensed and accredited) was so obscure. How important was flexibility? The college had no track record with off-campus operations or education on military installations. But their presentation had coherence, and, Johnson reasoned, the program would be tailor made. The Hammond Bay transfer policy was liberal—they would accept twelve credit hours from other institutions. The tuition would be $357 per credit hour.

Metropolitan University was a private university of twenty-five thousand students in the heart of the state capital, a forty-five-minute drive from Coastal. The university would bring to Coastal its successful experience in extending a wide range of educational services to an equally wide range of constituencies. Metropolitan's experience with adults, working students, and professionals, and its considerable resources, made an appealing combination. On the other hand, it was not clear that Metropolitan could offer a flexible program, because schools and departments within the university had trouble agreeing. The colleges of business and engineering seemed to be living in different worlds and speaking different languages. Although Metropolitan was anxious to come to Coastal and would bring rich resources, Johnson worried about the university's fragmentation. Metropolitan's transfer policy was moderately conservative—they accepted six hours of transfer credit. The tuition would be $300 per semester hour.

Southern State College was one of the smaller colleges in the State system, and only a fifteen-minute drive from Coastal. Although it had no experience with military education, it had a reputation of providing quality education to residents in the area, and engineering and business were its strongest graduate programs. The college was willing to respond flexibly to Coastal in developing a curriculum. Johnson was impressed by the fact that Southern expressed a commitment to use its own day faculty for the base program. In fact, prior to the presentation, Johnson was inclined to think that Southern was the solution to his problems. Afterward, he was far from sure: the dean of Southern's business school, representing the college, gave a talk that was poorly prepared and disorganized.

He was unable to give direct answers to many of the questions posed by the committee. He said he needed more information, indicating his willingness to return again after consultation. Southern State would allow six to nine hours of transfer credit from other institutions.

QUESTIONS FOR CONSIDERATION AND DISCUSSION

1. To what extent has Ronald Johnson appropriately assessed and determined the educational needs of employees at Coastal Military Installation? Are his assumptions and plans adequate? Are there categories of employees, or educational opportunities, that have been overlooked?
2. Review each of the institutional responses to Coastal's request for proposals. Given the evaluative criteria of reputation, flexibility, and cost, determine the rank of each institution's proposal. What are the strengths and weaknesses of each choice?
3. What advice would you give to the institution that ultimately receives the contract to offer the master's program at Coastal? What advice would you give Ronald Johnson as he and his team begin the implementation efforts surrounding the new program?

PROFILE #20: HOW MUCH ACCESS IS TOO MUCH ACCESS? (POLICY ISSUES)

Archer McPherson-Foote looked out the window at the trees beginning to change color as autumn approached. She turned to her three colleagues at the table and said, "OK. Let me review where we are now. I am going to meet the governor tomorrow morning and tell him he has to make a decision that will have a negative impact on a program he really cares about. Regardless of the decision he makes, the program is going to be different when the dust settles. And I'm the messenger. Is that about right?"

Tony Provenzano, the vice president for Administration at North Meridian State University, looked a bit uneasy as he replied to the university's president, "Well, Archer, that may be overstating it a bit, but, yes, we do not have any options that address all of the concerns that have arisen. I'm sorry, but there is no rabbit to pull out of the hat this time."

Edwina Roth, the vice president for Academic Affairs, was sitting across from Provenzano, and she nodded her head in agreement. "You know, this isn't a question of bad management, or of someone screwing up. There is no one to blame. It's just that things didn't work out the way we had anticipated."

The fourth person in the room, Les Austin, the university's vice president for Legislative Affairs, spoke up: "I could say almost the same thing for the legislature's position. At the beginning, this was everyone's favorite ornament on the Christmas tree: small cost, big impact. Now that the situation has changed and we face big costs and small impact, people have started to say they never thought the ornament was that pretty in the first place."

The president smiled grimly. "I think this is what they referred to at the New Presidents' Institute I attended in Washington, as the LOT-E option: choose the alternative which is Least Offensive to Everyone." She paused, and then continued, "Well, you know the drill. Let me hear all the options, and then we can attempt some systematic analysis. Let's get started."

BACKGROUND

When Jeremy Hubbard was elected governor of North Meridian in 2002, it was widely believed that his success could be attributed to his "new populism." He was a tireless advocate for universal outreach and access. The theme of his campaign could be summed up in two sentences he repeated frequently: "The services provided by this state should not be limited to those who know about them, or those who have easy access to them. Everyone should have access so that it is their choice to use them or not."

After his election, he moved quickly to implement his "universal access" pledges. His administration quickly focused on three areas in which to concentrate initial activities: health services, education, and public transportation. In the area of education, several areas were quickly identified where "access" was a problem: English as a second language, special education, and remediation services to K–12 students, and vocational education.

Hubbard knew that the services needed could and should be provided through local schools, and he planned a decentralized program to increase funds to school districts for those purposes. At the same time, he was convinced that the public higher education system should become more "accessible" to the state's growing population of groups for whom higher education institutions appeared to be complex and unfriendly, including non-English and limited-English speakers, the working poor, and "displaced" workers needing new training and skill development.

The Public Education System in North Meridian

North Meridian's public postsecondary education system was large and complex, with a flagship comprehensive university; three regional universities; separate medical, engineering, and law schools, each with its own campus; and six community colleges offering a variety of associate's degrees. The four universities were geographically situated throughout the state; enrollments in the postsecondary institutions had leveled off from their highs of the 1990s, and there was actually "excess capacity" on some campuses, so that an increased number of students could be accommodated.

The governor wanted to make visible inroads quickly, and he found that he had a unique opportunity to do so. North Meridian University, the state's flagship institution, was searching for a new president, and he would play an important role in the final decision. In April 2004, Hubbard used the press conference introducing Archer McPherson-Foote as the university's new president to also announce his plan for providing open access to postsecondary education for all citizens. "If you cannot come to us," he said, "we will come to you. Dr. McPherson-Foote has many goals for our great university, but she has assured me that providing access will be among her most important objectives."

Predictably, McPherson-Foote's first year was occupied with staffing issues and becoming acquainted with campus issues as priorities. Thus, the task of creating a plan to "provide access" was the responsibility of the governor's staff. The state's Higher Education Commissioner, Jason Fenton, a long-time associate of Governor Hubbard, was the "point person," and he was careful to keep McPherson-Foote and the other university and community college presidents apprised of the plan's development. When the governor's plan was issued in March 2004, there were few surprises; it was, as described in an editorial in *The Beacon*, the state's largest newspaper, "bold, comprehensive, ambitious, and—oh yes—targeted to population groups whose support would be extremely helpful in the Governor's reelection campaign." The report was titled: ACCESS: What Our Citizens Need, What North Meridian Will Provide: Educational Outreach Activities for the Twenty-First Century.

THE PLAN FOR NORTH MERIDIAN

The plan was innovative, remarkably simple in concept, and targeted to every citizen over thirty who had a high school diploma but lacked a higher degree or credential. There were five operational principles:

1. The program would be financed with funding from the state lottery which, by law, could only be used for "direct services" in areas of health, education, and social services.
2. Courses could be taught at any of the state's higher education facilities (and, in the absence of such facilities, at local schools) if there were sufficient demand and enrollment. Regardless of where the courses were taught, all courses offered under this program would have common titles, course numbering, and syllabi. Courses which were satisfactorily completed could be transferred to any public institution in the state.
3. Faculty members at all public institutions in the state could volunteer to teach these courses, or teaching could be assigned as part of workload if institutional enrollments could not support a full teaching load for particular faculty members.

4. Each institution providing a faculty member to teach a course would receive a lump sum for each faculty member involved. Funds received by institutions could be used with broad discretion, and were not tied to specific line items in institutional budgets.
5. Qualifying students could take up to ten courses through this program, and be charged only a $60 processing fee for each course, approximately 10 percent of what in-state tuition was.

SURGES IN ENROLLMENT AND TANGIBLE ACHIEVEMENTS

Almost a half century earlier, North Meridian had established a "GED" program for those who had never completed high school, and that program was very beneficial in helping reduce the rate of "habitual" unemployment. A tradition of low tuition for in-state residents had made it possible for many students from low income families to attend a postsecondary institution. But, for those who had graduated from high school, but had not obtained any education beyond that by the time they were thirty, there were few options, and no publicly funded opportunities. Thus, the appeal of the program was immediately evident, just as the governor and university president had envisioned.

Inquiries poured in, the program website "crashed" on several occasions, and of the forty-six courses offered during the first semester of implementation, only two had to be cancelled because they did not meet minimum enrollments. "We have a winner," McPherson-Foote enthusiastically wrote the governor, "but even more important, people who have had no options and no access, they are winners."

After two years, and in the last year of his term before he had to campaign for reelection, the program Governor Hubbard had begun was robust, and widely admired. In a presentation at the National Governors' Conference, he said: "We can be proud as Americans about how much access we have provided—to the poor, to minority group members, to women, to those with special needs—but the job will not be done until we have identified all bypassed groups, all those whose access has been limited or thwarted, and reached out to help them."

Indeed, North Meridian's educational outreach program seemed to have few detractors, and many supporters. The state's commissioner of higher education, Jason Fenton, lauded "the positive synergy among state higher education institutions to reach out to a group we have not thought enough about in the past, or done enough to help."

Fenton went on to identify four "mileposts of success":

- *Cost-effectiveness and increased institutional fiscal discretion:* The program incorporated enrollment fluctuations at institutions into its financial model by making it easy to redeploy a faculty member in a department or program with low enrollments, and have that person teach in the new program. When this type of reassignment occurred, the institution received a payment from the state's lottery revenues, which could be used for discretionary purposes.
- *Common course titles and numbers:* This practice made it easier for students to transfer credits and, when common syllabi were used, it was easier to hire temporary or adjunct faculty to teach, as less preparation would be needed.
- *New opportunities for previously bypassed groups:* In two years, nearly six thousand individuals had enrolled in one or more courses. Fifty-five percent were women, forty percent were people of color, and half had been unemployed at least once in the five years prior to enrollment.
- *Use of lottery funds for direct services:* In the decade since the lottery had been approved in North Meridian, there had been little tangible evidence that funds were being used to help people, rather than to expand the state's bureaucracy. This program affected "real" people, giving them opportunities that they had not previously had.

WHAT HAVE WE GAINED?

Hubbard was reelected, as expected, with the education program included among his positive accomplishments. The governor had hoped to turn his attention in his second term to expanding the state's economy, and to manage rapidly rising health care costs, but in his sixth year as governor, concerns about the ACCESS program surfaced and, within months, the ACCESS program seemed to be foundering, and the governor was fighting to keep it alive.

The first public indication of concern about the ACCESS program came from the Lottery Oversight Commission, a bipartisan group of eleven members who were not involved in running the state lottery, but who were charged with reviewing the allocation of funds to ensure they were consistent with the lottery's charter to "provide direct services." The Commission's annual report stated:

> We view with concern the present allocation system for the ACCESS program. We acknowledge that the lottery funds do enable a needy and worthy group of citizens the opportunity to take courses which can help them earn a degree or obtain employment. But, the funds which are allocated for the program from the lottery are paid directly to the institutions which can then use those funds for any purposes they wish. There is no direct link between the actual costs of the ACCESS program and the money paid to the institutions. The fundamental policy must be reviewed with an eye toward reformulation.

When the commission's report was published, McPherson-Foote, anticipating a phone call from the governor, asked Edwina Roth, the vice president for Academic Affairs, to prepare a justification for the present allocation system. Roth's "talking points" (see Exhibit 5.2) were based on pragmatism and the hard-core realities of a system operating with many constraints, not an educational justification for the program and its purposes. Governor Hubbard used those arguments in a written response to the Lottery Oversight Commission, and then concluded, somewhat curtly, that it was "entirely appropriate to use lottery funds for these purposes."

A second problem with the ACCESS program arose when a political adversary of the governor released some troubling data. Gene Ward, a longtime member of the state senate and a likely candidate for governor in the next election, called a press conference to "present some facts" to the citizens of the state.

EXHIBIT 5.2:   EDWINA ROTH'S "TALKING POINTS" MEMO

1. There are relatively few sources of discretionary funds in the higher education budget. Being able to generate some discretionary funds is a big "plus." The prospect of this was a big incentive in persuading faculty to become involved in teaching in the ACCESS program.

2. Without some of the cost efficiencies of common syllabi and course numbering, and the opportunity for "redeploying" faculty, the ACCESS program could never have been launched.

3. Redeployment of faculty, essentially the opportunity to assign faculty to teach in the ACCESS program if there were not sufficient enrollments in the courses they normally taught, avoided the prospect of having to eliminate faculty positions.

4. The money spent on a per-person-per course basis was lower in the ACCESS program than in the degree programs in campus programs.

Ward reported that in nearly five years the ACCESS program had achieved few of its objectives. He cited the following:

• Less than 20 percent of students who had participated in the program had actually enrolled in a degree program.
• The attrition rate for students in the ACCESS program was twice that of students enrolled in the state's other postsecondary institutions.
• The average class size in the ACCESS program was eleven, compared with twenty-eight for lower division courses at state institutions.

Ward said, "What does all of this tell us? It tells us of a massive giveaway of state funds because the governor believes in access. Access for what purpose? Access with what intended results? These questions can't be answered because there are no answers. This has been a program filled with lofty language, but no real goals. The governor wants to bring educational access to everyone, but he can't tell us how the state will be better off as a result. Yes, more people have access now, but how much has it cost and what have we gained?"

Abstract Goals, Tangible Results

A seasoned and pragmatic politician, Governor Hubbard was not surprised to have one of his highly visible programs criticized, but he was surprised at how quickly support for the ACCESS program had waned, and how little tangible evidence there was to demonstrate that the program was important, and working as had been intended. "What my critics do not understand," he said at his press conference to refute Ward's assertions, "is that ACCESS is both a program and a pledge. If something in the program isn't working we have to fix it because we certainly cannot go back on our pledge." Despite that bold statement, the overall loss of support for the program would necessitate some changes, and strategists in the governor's office and at the university began to consider what could be done, what could be modified or eliminated, what must be retained, and what options were possible.

To help him prepare for the political battles he would have to undertake, the governor turned to Archer McPherson-Foote to help organize the "educational response" he would need to propose to keep the ACCESS program intact. He might have to compromise on some issues, but he was determined to keep the overall program viable. He called her, and told her what he needed.

After several hours of discussion with her colleagues, McPherson-Foote said, "I guess we have considered this from every angle. Let me mull this over for a while, and I will let you know what I've decided." She looked at the list of options she had written down as they had talked (see Table 5.2), and said with a wry smile on her face, "So, what is LOT-E?"

TABLE 5.2: OPTIONS FOR CONSIDERATION

	Proposal	*Explanation*
Option 1	Scale back geographically	Continue present policy of offering courses, but only in identified "target outreach areas" (such as locations where no course is offered in a fifty-mile radius).
Option 2	Scale back programmatically	Continue present policy of offering courses, but only for entry-level required courses at the associate's level (that is, general education, skill proficiency, and critical writing and thinking).
Option 3	Develop a lower cost alternative delivery system	Develop and implement a distance learning capability using both synchronous and asynchronous modalities, and eventually discontinue on site instructional activities except at established institutional settings.
Option 4	Outsource programs and provide subsidies	Establish "outsource" contracts with private accredited for-profit and nonprofit institutions with the state subsidizing the difference between public tuition rates and the rates charged by the private institutions.
Option 5	Reduce reliance on lottery by raising student costs or establishing a county surcharge based on student enrollments	Ask local communities to share the per-person expenses that exceed the established public tuition rates.
Option 6	Eliminate use of full-time faculty, and use only part-time faculty at lower rates	Hire only part-time faculty to teach in the outreach program, and lobby the legislature to waive the requirement that part-time faculty receive certain fringe benefits (notably health insurance and a prorated professional development allocation).

QUESTIONS FOR CONSIDERATION AND DISCUSSION

1. What are the strengths of the ACCESS program, and what are the limitations or drawbacks? To what extent has the program accomplished its stated objective?
2. Review the "talking points" memo in Exhibit 5.2. To what extent do you agree with these points? How might points be edited or added to make a more persuasive case?
3. Review the various options presented in Table 5.2. To what extent do you agree that these are the options? What additional options exist? What option should be chosen, and why?
4. To what extent should higher education be an entitlement? How do institutions reconcile universal access with individual merit and accomplishment?

PROFILE #21: THE BASE OF THE PYRAMID (POLICY ISSUES)

"You don't get it, Kevin. You just don't get it," Maria Conterra said, a hint of exasperation in her voice. As executive director of New Dorset's system of nine community colleges, Conterra was used to being listened to, not challenged. In this meeting, Kevin Warrenton, the governor's budget director, had just told her that her success in reducing the drop-out rate in the community colleges was not a success at all, but a "mammoth sinkhole" based on arbitrarily increasing the number of credits needed to obtain an associate's degree. Conterra believed she had provided an adequate explanation, backed up by student completion data, of how and why the changes that had occurred were beneficial to students, and to the state.

Warrenton, she felt, could not see beyond the "cost per unit" mentality of a budget director trying to stretch budget dollars to their limits. He looked at cost per inmate in the state's correctional system, cost per bed in state-controlled hospitals, cost per mile for maintaining state highways and bridges, and cost per academic credit in the same way: costs should increase in a predictable way based on the rate of inflation and the availability of funding distributed proportionally across a particular sector. It was unreasonable and irrational, he had said, to increase the instructional budget for community colleges at two or three times the rate of increase for the instructional budget of the state's public universities and colleges.

Warrenton looked at his watch, acting as if the meeting was nearly over, and Conterra felt she had to try again to explain why the "credit issue" was so important. "Kevin," she said, "please give me a few minutes to describe the academic progress of our community college students."

Background

Two-thirds of the population of New Dorset lives in four sprawling urban areas, and six of the nine community colleges are in those areas. Since the mid-1990s enrollments in community colleges have increased at a consistently higher rate than in the state's public universities and colleges. Originally funded by local communities (counties), the nine community colleges now received most of their funding from the state. Legislators from areas of the state where there are no accessible community colleges for their constituents argue that funding for the universities and colleges should serve everyone in the state rather than just those in a particular county.

Funding from the state for the three postsecondary systems (the university, the state colleges, and the community colleges) was allocated in two ways: general institutional support and instructional support. Instructional support was based on a generic FTE (full-time equivalent) formula, but the FTE funding was highest for the university, followed by the state colleges, and then by the community colleges. The difference in the FTE allocations was justified for the university and colleges because of the greater demands for research and scholarship and because of the many graduate programs offered. The FTE model in use for several decades was based on 124 credits required for a bachelor's degree and 60 credits required for an associate's degree.

Maria Conterra had spent her entire professional career in community colleges, and had been a faculty member, academic dean, and president in New Dorset for fifteen years before being named executive director of the community college system in 2003. As an advocate for community colleges and community college students, Conterra had spoken out against a system which she believed was biased against the two-year institutions. The board of trustees and the governor had told her to focus her attention on three areas:

- Managing and developing the extensive part-time faculty
- Reducing the proportion of part-time students and the time to program completion
- Reducing high drop-out and "failure to complete" rates

After several years, Conterra believed she had made some progress in each area, but it was painfully slow. She also felt that the poor quality of public secondary schools was having a devastating impact on the community colleges, and she was being forced to deal with their failures and deficiencies.

A DETERIORATING EDUCATIONAL INFRASTRUCTURE

As was true in other states in the region, the population demographics of New Dorset had begun to change in the 1950s and the percent of state residents living in urban areas increased. In the 1980 census, for example, 45 percent of the population lived in four "metropolitan areas"; in the 2000 census, it had increased to just over 60 percent. Most of the available indicators showed a steady decline in the quality of life. Unemployment rates, the percent of people living below the poverty level, the number of single-parent families, and the percent of school dropouts increased annually, and some were at twice the level of rural communities in the state. Urban decay and the decline of the service infrastructure had come to be the norm, not the aberration.

This was particularly evident in the deterioration of the urban school systems attended by 75 percent of the state's students. In a study completed in 2006, two of the four urban school districts in New Dorset were among seventeen of the fifty largest school districts in the United States whose graduation rates were 50 percent or lower. Even more alarming than the dismal data about high school drop-outs were the results of studies done about high school graduates' "readiness" for college. "Readiness" was defined as having passed (with a grade of C or better) five courses required by the state Board of Education in order to be eligible for admission to a postsecondary institution. The mean percentage of students who met the "readiness" requirement in New Dorset's two largest cities was 40 percent as indicated in Table 5.3.

TABLE 5.3: PERCENTAGE OF PUBLIC SCHOOL 12TH GRADE GRADUATES COMPLETING COURSES (WITH A GRADE OF "C" OR BETTER) REQUIRED FOR ENTERING STUDENTS IN POSTSECONDARY INSTITUTIONS IN NEW DORSET

	1997	2001	2005
New Dorset Metropolitan Population Center (MPC) # 1	42.9%	41.6%	37.3%
New Dorset MPC #2	46.4%	43.0%	43.1%

Pragmatically, this meant that if a person looked at a room of one hundred tenth-grade students in one of those urban schools, fewer than fifty of them would graduate from high school. Of those (approximately) fifty students, only twenty would be eligible for admission to one of the state's postsecondary institutions. Of course, the drop-out rate was lower and the "readiness" rate was higher in suburban and rural schools, but the students in those schools comprised only 25 percent of the high school population.

A poor-quality secondary education system had an impact on all three postsecondary institutions, but it had a particularly adverse effect on community college enrollments. And the data indicated that there were no "quick fixes" or "easy solutions" on the horizon. Thus, the state of New Dorset faced an enormous challenge: the number of high school–age students was increasing, but the number of students eligible to enroll in postsecondary institutions was decreasing, especially in the community colleges.

ENROLLMENTS IN THE COMMUNITY COLLEGES

The nine community colleges in New Dorset were reorganized under one central administrative structure in 1986 in order to create more centralized policies and procedures, and by 1994 there were uniform academic and curricular standards, equitable across-the-system salary ranges for faculty and staff, and a master plan for program growth. Although there were inevitable differences in program quality and reputation among the colleges, New Dorset's community college system was respected, and had produced enviable results when compared with other state systems.

In 1996, for example, fifty-two percent of students who had enrolled in certificate, licensure, or degree programs in 1992 had achieved their objectives; this had increased to 54 and 57 percent respectively in 2000 and 2004. These numbers were somewhat deceptive because a third of all students who enrolled

TABLE 5.4: PERCENT OF NEWLY ENROLLED STUDENTS BY ADMISSIONS CATEGORY, NEW DORSET COMMUNITY COLLEGES

Category	1997	2001	2005	2008 (Projected)
Eligible students (those who have graduated from high school and passed the state mandated courses documenting "readiness to learn" with grades of C or better)	26%	22%	19%	16%
Provisional students (those who have graduated from high school in the last four years, but have not yet met the "readiness to learn" requirements)	17	20	19	22
Non-matriculated (students between the ages of 18 and 24 who have attended high school through the tenth grade (but have not graduated) may enroll in the remediation program which provides preparation for GED exams or preparation for proficiency exams in the required subject areas of academic "readiness")	23	21	23	21
Exempt (students 25 and older are exempt from the high school graduation and "readiness to learn" requirements, but must enroll in and complete at least one remediation course each semester, and pass one proficiency exam each year)	34	36	39	41

were "undeclared" and had not specified a program objective when they enrolled.

Students were admitted to community colleges in four categories, as shown in Table 5.4.

In practical terms, this meant that 74 percent of all newly enrolled students in 1997 needed to enroll in, or pass a proficiency exam in, one or more subjects. That trend continued as the percent of eligible students declined. Enrollment projections for 2008 suggested that 84 percent of new enrolled students would not meet the eligibility requirement.

Before becoming executive director, Conterra had served as dean for Academic Support Services for the community college system, and felt that she understood the causes of the low completion rates, and knew what strategies to use to reduce the number of student dropouts. In one of her early reports to the board of trustees (who were appointed by the governor) she wrote:

> Here's some context for you: According to the American Association of Community Colleges (www.aacc.nche.edu), the average age of community college students is twenty-nine; the majority of students are over the age of twenty-two; nearly 20 percent are single parents; almost 60 percent are women; nearly 40 percent are first-generation college students; and 50 percent of both full- and part-time students work full-time while attending community colleges.
>
> The demographic diversity of our students—especially the number of adult learners who may not be fully prepared and for whom college attendance is not their only (or even first) priority— contributes to our retention and persistence goals. Indeed, when we admit students who are not academically prepared to do the work, we should not be surprised when they *can't* do the work, and then fail. If we admit students to degree or certificate programs who are not "ready" to do college-level work, it is our responsibility and obligation to offer courses that will prepare them to adequately meet our standards. This is a remedial function, but we must do for them what their prior education did not do.

Under Conterra's leadership, the remedial course structure was revamped, more sections of each remedial course were added, testing and equivalency options were increased, and tutorial services and learning labs were expanded significantly.

The Costs of Remediation

The Remediation Program in the Community Colleges was designed to be congruent with the state's mandatory Readiness for College requirements. To be eligible for admission, student had to demonstrate competence in the following areas:

- Critical thinking
- Science in today's world
- Analysis and interpretation
- Modern mathematics
- History and culture

Competence could be demonstrated in one of three ways: (1) passing a high school course in the subject area with a grade of C or better; (2) passing a community college course in the subject area at the 100 (introductory) level; (3) passing a competency exam (offered by the community college) in the subject area with a grade of 72 or better.

To prepare students for the 100-level courses, the community colleges had created a corresponding group of "0XX" courses which would help students establish a foundation that would increase their prospects for passing the 100-level courses. The "0XX" courses could be taken for credit, but did not count in the sixty-credit requirement for associate's degrees. Students could, if necessary, take each "0XX" course twice.

Students could also take four different workshop courses for credit:

- Reading for Understanding
- Writing and Revising
- Mathematics Review
- English as a Second Language

These initiatives began to show positive results, and the number of students who were "fully eligible" after completing fifteen credits rose by 15 percent after three years; equally noteworthy, the drop-out rate among students who became "fully eligible" began to decline. Conterra and her faculty and administrative colleagues were elated, but these positive changes came at a high cost, and Conterra knew that a financial reckoning would eventually occur.

What Is Required? Sixty Credits? Eighty Credits?

There were two academic yardsticks which the community colleges used to validate the success of the remediation efforts: the increase in the proportion of students who were "fully eligible" and the decrease in the drop-out rate among those students. The downside, however, was glaring: since the implementation of the remediation program, the average number of credits students had earned at the time of graduation had increased from sixty (the minimum requirement) to sixty-eight, a 12 percent increase.

In testimony before the legislative committee on education a year before, Conterra had said, "As educational quality in high schools decreases, it is inevitable that the number of credits students need to complete their work in a community college increases. It is the 'remedial' credits added to the sixty-credit degree requirement that enables students to succeed."

This provoked a strong reaction from some legislators concerned about spiraling budgets for the community colleges. "What you are telling us," one legislator said, "is that you want us to pay for seventy or even eighty credits for a degree that is supposed to cost the taxpayers only sixty credits." Similar legislative reactions, critical newspaper editorials, and defensive explanations and denials from secondary school officials brought the issue to the governor and his aides. The governor asked his budget director, Kevin Warrenton, to meet with Maria Conterra. "Ask her to explain why this is happening, and whether the number of credits is going to continue to increase."

The Base of the Pyramid

"Our goal," Conterra said, "is to graduate people with an associate's degree. For most of them, an associate's degree will open doors to employment and decent salaries. For many them, they will be the first in their families to obtain a degree beyond high school. They can't get there by wishing, and we can't get them there by hoping."

Warrenton's expression softened. "I admire your goals and respect your success, but if we have to provide funds for seventy or more credits in order to award a sixty-credit degree, we are spending more than we have and more than we said it would cost. Besides, I worry too about our candor in saying that we offer a sixty-credit degree when we know that a significant number or students can't—and won't—earn a degree with that number of credits."

Conterra said, "Kevin, if you build a pyramid and want its apex to be high, you start with a broad base. The ancient Egyptians knew the formula: the higher the apex, the broader the base. If the educational apex isn't high enough or stable enough with a base of sixty credits, we need to broaden the base of the pyramid, and that's what we are doing."

QUESTIONS FOR CONSIDERATION AND DISCUSSION

1. What do you believe to be the role of community colleges in providing access and opportunity to adult learners in higher education?
2. To what extent are Kevin Warrenton's concerns reasonable? What underlying problems do the increased credit hours pose to the state?
3. What advice would you provide Maria Conterra and her colleagues on making a compelling and persuasive case for maintaining and increasing funding?
4. To what extent are the issues of remediation an indication of the quality of K–12 schools? Individual adult learners? Policymakers? Employers? Others?

PROFILE #22: HOW TO ACHIEVE AN APPROPRIATE BALANCE (POLICY ISSUES)

Driving to campus, Leah Van Hoosen realized she had never actually arrived at her office before 6:00 AM, and, for a brief moment, even wondered if the building would be unlocked at such an early hour. Finding the custodial and facility services staff still in the building, Leah relaxed a bit, for she didn't relish the idea of being alone in the vast building by herself for at least an hour before others would slowly start to trickle in. Her mind was already distracted enough. At 9:00 she had her first strategy-setting meeting

with a new, ambitious young dean who had proposed an innovative approach to serving adult learners in his unit. She wanted
to make a good impression, but she realized that what was being
proposed was going to require up-front investment at a time when
it seemed the political winds on campus were blowing in a decidedly different direction.

Urban State University and Medical Center (USUMC) had
grown rapidly in its relatively young forty-five-year history. Like
other urban public institutions, it had roots in the city for decades
prior to its "official" opening during a time of rapid expansion in
American higher education. Initially it operated in various buildings—some dilapidated, others dating back to the 1800s, and precious few that were built brand new at the time—and occupied
a part of the city that showed signs of urban blight. USUMC was
also the site of the state's only medical school, which had been
in operation for nearly fifty years prior to the campus's exis-
tence. USUMC's early students were mainly local, nearly all first-
generation, primarily nontraditional, and were often thought to
be students who lacked the motivation or preparation to attend
the two other state-supported residential, traditional, and presumably more prestigious flagship campuses.

Over the years, USUMC rapidly grew to become a true pow-
erhouse in the state and a model of how urban higher education
institutions, and, indeed, all colleges and universities, must evolve
to meet the needs of their stakeholders. By the early 2000s, the
institution had developed over twelve academic units, served nearly
thirty thousand students in a state-of-the-art campus that housed
several new buildings, and was part of an ever-sprawling medical
complex. It increasingly attracted better-prepared first-year, full-
time freshmen students and had grown in reputation thanks, in
part, to significant external funding driven by its many programs
oriented toward medicine and life sciences. In spite of these
changes, USUMC had many legacy elements as part of its institutional portfolio, and none was more prominent than the number
of adult learners the institution continued to serve. In fact, nearly
55 percent of undergraduates were over the age of twenty-five,
and many in the community still viewed USUMC as "their" institution—one that provided access and opportunities for those unable
to attend other colleges or go to school on a full-time basis.

In 2004, a new executive vice president and provost, William Fulton, was recruited to USUMC to replace Sally DuFore, a fifteen-year veteran of the post, who was arguably instrumental in helping to shape the expansion of the campus, including several award-winning programs focused on student learning. One jewel in the crown was USUMC's Center for Teaching Excellence, a unit that offered workshops, consultations, and assistance to faculty on a variety of teaching-learning related initiatives. These included sessions on instructional design and development, distance learning, classroom management techniques, and scholarship of teaching and learning activities. Sally held the center in high regard, and often ensured that Leah and her team were showcased prominently in faculty recruitment efforts, the institution's annual report, and even at national meetings where center faculty often served as presenters.

When Sally retired and William was recruited to USUMC, the campus climate began to change. William, a prominent biochemist with a strong record of externally funded, discipline-specific grants, was specifically brought in to help raise the research productivity in the nonmedical units on campus, and, as many of the faculty quickly understood, was also chosen primarily for his ability to go "toe to toe" with the Medical Center faculty and administrators who often exerted great influence over decisions at USUMC. One of William's first moves was to convince the president and board of trustees to reorder the campus mission so that research was placed before teaching in the mission statement. This, he felt, would signify to faculty and external stakeholders USUMC's commitment to becoming much more active in research.

Suddenly, it seemed, most of the new initiatives announced from central administration were all rooted in research. Promotion and tenure criteria were revised to reflect more rigorous scholarly contributions and competitive external funding. New faculty hires were given significant start-up packages to launch their research agendas and several were assigned teaching loads of one section per year. This posed some friction within departments, as faculty who had been at USUMC felt that their campus was changing around them, and that William and others in leadership positions did not sufficiently value the teaching mission of the campus.

As a politically savvy administrator, William understood the faculty's concerns but acknowledged that USUMC "must now assert its rightful place in the state's higher education landscape" by enhancing its reputation through greater research activities. This, he indicated, would require a change in faculty roles and rewards, one that would occur incrementally but had the potential to shape USUMC's future in profound ways. To support both the research and teaching missions of the campus, William proposed—and several academic unit deans ultimately embraced—a new model for faculty work.

The newly emerging structure of faculty work tended to place the undergraduate teaching responsibilities on the following types of faculty: tenured faculty who were not research active, full-time lecturers (whose primary responsibility was to teach and provide advising to students) and an increasingly large cadre of adjunct instructors who were hired on a per-course contract. Research-active tenured faculty and all tenure-track faculty hired since 2005 taught precious few undergraduate courses; they either taught primarily at the graduate level or had their time "bought out" by grants—all done in name of providing them a platform to conduct research that would lead to external funding, enhanced reputation, and, ultimately, help USUMC attract even better-prepared students.

Leah Van Hoosen understood the rationale for the enhanced research emphasis at USUMC, but this shift in mission had direct implications for the Center for Teaching Excellence. For starters, her base funding had been cut by over 25 percent in the past two years and she was unable to fill a professional-level instructional designer position when a colleague left last year. Reallocation of the center's funding cuts was provided to the newly formed Center for Research Excellence to expand undergraduate research efforts—again, a worthy goal, but one that was, as one of her staff put it, "coming off of our backs."

In 2008, a new dean, Feng Chen, was hired to lead the School of Professional Studies (SPS), a unit that housed continuing education and the undergraduate general and professional studies baccalaureate degree. Recognizing very quickly that SPS faculty were not very research active and were likely to never rise to the level of prominence that William and others would desire, Feng developed an innovative strategy for SPS. USUMC served an area where less than 20 percent of all adults over the age of twenty-five had a bachelor's degree. This was a statistic that was not lost on Feng, nor the new-entrant competitors who were increasingly populating the marketplace and who aggressively marketed online and shorted courses to help adults finish their degrees.

A centerpiece of Feng's strategy was to offer the entire general and professional studies bachelor's degree online and to use adjunct instructors to teach all of the courses. The modest number of full-time SPS faculty would shift their roles to become "educational managers" of the adjunct faculty, and would ensure consistency, oversight of courses, and serve as a resource to adjuncts and students alike. This would permit SPS to rapidly expand its offerings without adding significant cost to the base budget. Feng hoped to roll out this new model within one academic year, as early discussions with SPS faculty yielded tremendous excitement about the prospect of taking such a bold and innovative approach to their work. What made this even more exciting was the fact that SPS would be the first unit at USUMC to offer an entire degree program online. Other units offered certificate programs, a select graduate program or two, and an array of disparate courses online (including some in SPS), but there had never been a full undergraduate degree program offered in this manner.

When Feng presented the idea to Leah, she was enthused. After all, she thought, what SPS is proposing to do would expand USUMC's teaching impact on its service area and beyond, especially as it relates to a legacy stakeholder: adult learners. Leah suggested meeting with Feng later that week to develop a strategy to recruit, orient, and develop the adjunct faculty to serve this program. Once the strategy was fleshed out a bit, they could both propose it to William in the hopes of getting the green light, and some campus-level investment, for the approach.

As Leah sat in her office at this early hour, she yawned. All night long, she had wrestled with conflicting thoughts. How would she be able to help Feng and SPS when she had a hard enough time assisting the other eleven academic units with their faculty development needs? How would she be able to convince William that this innovative idea, one not rooted in a research initiative, was worthy of investment from the campus? Would the concept of using full-time faculty as "educational managers" of adjunct instructors even work? All of these thoughts swirled in her head as she waited for her computer to start. When it was fully on, she opened her SPS Strategy file and began making additional notes. I'd better capture all of my concerns and challenges before the meeting with Feng, Leah thought as she began typing away at the keyboard.

Questions for Consideration and Discussion

1. What are some of the competing and coexisting tensions that the USUMC campus is facing? How and to what extent do these tensions affect the institution's ability to serve adult learners? Can USUMC achieve an appropriate balance between its various mission foci?
2. What are the strengths and challenges of employing large numbers of adjunct instructors to augment the teaching requirements at institutions? What should be the role of full-time faculty in such an environment? How can adjunct instructors be best supported?
3. What are some of the instructional and other considerations that must be made in transitioning an adult-oriented program, such as the general and professional studies bachelor's degree, to entirely online delivery? What are the implications for the institution? For faculty? For learners?
4. What advice can you provide to Leah and Feng as they develop their strategy to support faculty and adult learners in SPS? What are strengths of their approach? What concerns do you envision? How should the case be made for additional support or investment from central administration to sustain this initiative?

Summary

Each profile in this chapter is necessarily structured to be open-ended, thereby permitting readers to analyze, reflect on, and consider how they might address similar issues in their own institutional context. We can, however, identify some common themes in these profiles and provide a brief discussion of how to better understand and support adult learners. Some of the *policy issues* include providing access while managing enrollment and other resource constraints; establishing criteria for evaluating adult learning programs; monitoring and improving efficiency and effectiveness of adult learning programs; and striking a balance between capacity, delivery method, and quality of offerings.

Many colleges and universities struggle over such issues as the tensions between centralization and decentralization, autonomy and control, consistency and flexibility, political and pragmatic decision making; on-campus, distance, and community-based teaching and learning; and mission differentiation. *The Weakest Link* encapsulates many of these, and highlights the challenges inherent in operating multiple locations or distribution channels under the banner of the same "brand." In doing so, reputation management issues of the people, programs, and impacts of the institution are of paramount concern. Similar dynamics are also evident in a related profile, *How to Achieve an Appropriate Balance*, which focuses on the role of distance learning and adjunct faculty, and how each are considered against the backdrop of an institution with a changing mission and culture.

In large, complex higher education systems, rivalry among and between campuses of the same system are frequently reported, and an internal hierarchy or pecking-order is often an unintended, yet real, outcome of this dynamic. Senior leaders can set the tone by outlining standards required of all programs, regardless of location or delivery method. They can also help in shaping and creating cultures, structures, reporting relationships, and controls that provide systemic uniformity where required, and localized individuality where desired.

Whereas *The Weakest Link* focused on the competitive aspects within an organization, *Coastal Military Installation* identified how institutions compete with one another in attracting potential students to their offerings. In this profile, viewed from the end-user decision makers' perspective, tough choices were evident when determining which course of action to pursue. Institutional leaders can best serve the needs of community and corporate partners by creating mechanisms to routinely assess their needs. They can also garner interest in the institution from these valuable external stakeholders by inviting their participation in the life of the institution by asking representatives from these settings to serve on boards of advisors, provide opportunities for students to participate in experiential learning (such as through internships or service learning), and showcasing the linkages between the institution's mission and purpose to the needs of external partners. Similarly, issues of access, responsiveness, and ensuring that external stakeholders understand the multifaceted challenges of college and university environments are explored in the profiles *How Much Access Is Too Much Access* and *The Base of the Pyramid*.

The *policy issues* presented in these profiles are representative of just a few of the many possibilities and eventualities in supporting adult learners. Please refer to the Action Planning and Readings and Resources sections that follow to help you and enhance understanding of these issues in your own institutional context.

ACTION PLANNING

- Based on information presented in the preceding profiles, what are similar *policy* issues related to adult learners at your college or university?
- What is your college or university doing especially well to understand and support *policy* issues related to adult learners?
- In what ways can your college or university improve its efforts to understand and support *policy* issues related to adult learners?
- Where might support for improvement efforts be garnered? To what extent would there be any resistance to such efforts?
- What are immediate next steps? What are longer-term considerations?
- Other resources, suggestions, or ideas?

READINGS AND RESOURCES

The following readings and resources are provided to expand knowledge on a particular *policy issue* related to adult learners in higher education. Each was selected because it expands on a concept, idea, or approach highlighted in one or more profiles. A more comprehensive bibliography is included at the conclusion of this book.

Alexander, F. K., and Ehrenberg, R. G. (Eds.). Maximizing resources: Universities, public policy, and revenue production. *New Directions for Institutional Research, 119.* San Francisco: Jossey-Bass, 2003.

Amey, M. J. (Ed.). Across educational sectors. *New Directions for Community Colleges, 139.* San Francisco: Jossey-Bass, 2007.

Anctil, E. J. Selling higher education: Marketing and advertising America's colleges and universities. *ASHE Higher Education Report, 34*(2). San Francisco: Jossey- Bass, 2008.

Aslanian, C. B. *Adult students today.* New York: The College Board, 2001.

Astin, A. W., Keup, J. R., and Lindholm, J. A. A decade of changes in undergraduate education: A national study of system "transformation." *Review of Higher Education, 25*(2), 141–162, 2002.

Burke, J. C. (Ed.). *Achieving accountability in higher education: Balancing public, academic, and market demands.* San Francisco: Jossey-Bass, 2004.

Crady, T., and Sumner, J. (Eds.). Key issues in new student enrollment. *New Directions for Student Services, 118.* San Francisco: Jossey-Bass, 2007.

Dickeson, R. C. *Prioritizing academic programs and services: Reallocating resources to achieve strategic balance.* San Francisco: Jossey-Bass, 1999.

Dotolo, L. G., and Noftsinger, J. B., Jr. (Eds.). Leveraging resources through partnerships. *New Directions for Higher Education, 120.* San Francisco: Jossey-Bass, 2002.

Flint, T. A., Zakos, P., and Frey, R. *Best practices in adult learning: A self-evaluation workbook for colleges and universities.* Dubuque, IA: Kendall/ Hunt, 2002.

Johnstone, S. M., Ewell, P., and Paulson, K. *Student learning as academic currency.* Washington, DC: American Council on Education, 2002.

King, J. E., Anderson, E. L, and Corrigan, M. E. (Eds.). Changing student attendance patterns: Challenges for policy and practice. *New Directions for Higher Education, 121.* San Francisco: Jossey-Bass, 2003.

Kinser, K. From main street to wall street: For-profit higher education. *AHSE Higher Education Report, 31*(5). San Francisco: Jossey-Bass, 2006.

Lapovsky, L., and Klinger, D. (Eds.). Strategic financial challenges for higher education: How to achieve quality, accountability, and innovation. *New Directions for Higher Education, 140.* San Francisco: Jossey-Bass, 2008.

Massey, W. F. *Honoring the trust: Quality and cost containment in higher education.* Bolton, MA: Anker, 2003.

Spangler, M. S. (Ed.). Developing successful partnerships with business and the community. *New Directions for Community Colleges, 119.* San Francisco: Jossey-Bass, 2002.

Townsend, B. K., and Dougherty, K. J. (Eds.). Community college missions in the 21st century. *New Directions for Community Colleges, 136.* San Francisco: Jossey-Bass, 2007.

CHAPTER SIX

ANALYZING AND IMPROVING COLLEGE AND UNIVERSITY ENVIRONMENTS FOR ADULT LEARNERS

After reading about, reflecting on, and analyzing the many issues related to adult learners in colleges and universities, presented through profiles in the preceding chapters, this chapter now asks you to more closely examine adult learning issues in your own environment. We have developed a framework—Prepare, Research, Plan, Implement—to accomplish this task. Under each part of the framework, there are specific, often sequential action items to consider. For those who desire a truly comprehensive and logical process, we suggest following each action item in sequence. Others, however, may benefit from considering the framework as embodying characteristics or principles of good practice in analyzing and improving environments for adult learners—that is, action items that need not necessarily be followed sequentially, but rather referenced as general guidelines for analysis and improvement efforts.

Regardless of how you use this framework, it is best to employ an approach to understanding and supporting adult learners that: (1) aligns with the institution's mission and context; (2) involves key leaders and institutional stakeholders; (3) uses an evidence-based approach to decision making; (4) engages in thoughtful, deliberate planning and implementation; and (5) evaluates and disseminates lessons learned from adult-centric initiatives. We hope the following framework will assist you in those efforts. Part I of the framework begins with how a college or university can

Prepare for its improvement efforts; Part II highlights the *Research* needed to understand adult learners; Part III outlines how to *Plan* for appropriate adult-centric interventions; finally, Part IV describes how to *Implement* improvements for adult learners.

PART I: PREPARE

Action items in the *Prepare* phase of the framework include the following:

- Determine the need and make the case for adult learners
- Establish level of analysis and project goals
- Clarify the broader context for adult learners
- Secure appropriate sponsorship
- Form a committee or task force

DETERMINE THE NEED AND MAKE THE CASE FOR ADULT LEARNERS

Although it is tempting for many well-intentioned individuals and leaders to want to enact changes quickly to support adult learners, it is necessary to first lay the foundation and prepare colleagues and others for such changes. The first step in the process, therefore, is to determine the need and make the case for adult learner initiatives. Diagnostic questions at this step include:

- What evidence suggests a need to understand and support adult learners?
- To what extent is there individual or collective advocacy for adult learners among faculty, staff, and other stakeholders?
- How have enrollment patterns changed over time to reflect an increase in adult learners?
- To what extent have changes to the competitive marketplace impacted interest in adult learners?
- Has leadership support for adult learners been explicit, implicit, or nonexistent?
- Have new programs or services been developed or considered for adult learners?
- Was there a critical event—or series of events—that brought the issue of adult learners to the forefront?

- Are we interested in enhancing and improving our environments for adult learners because of continuous quality improvement, accreditation, or other similar reasons?

These are representative questions to help determine the need for focusing on adult learner issues. Based on the answers, a sound case can be made for analyzing and improving environments for adult learners. To provide focus and clarity to such a case requires establishing a level of analysis and specific project goals.

ESTABLISH LEVEL OF ANALYSIS AND PROJECT GOALS

Ideally, understanding and supporting adult learners would be ubiquitous throughout all of higher education. Pragmatically, however, we must focus our tasks and efforts on a specific level of analysis. College and university structures can be complex and multifaceted. For overly simplistic purposes, we can establish the analysis around three broad levels: (1) department or program; (2) academic or service unit; and (3) campus or institution/system. Depending on the reader's interests, needs, scope of authority and responsibility, ability to influence, and the specific context, an appropriate level for analyzing and improving adult initiatives should be chosen.

After the level of analysis has been identified, it is necessary to outline project goals. What, specifically do you hope to accomplish in analyzing and improving the environment for adult learners at this particular level? Are you seeking to make enhancements to existing programs or services? Potentially launch or expand new ones? Encourage a change in individual, departmental, or institutional behavior? Respond to a specific inquiry, issue, or competitive threat? In determining answers to such questions, you will need to sketch out project goals that are specific, measurable, attainable, realistic, and timely. After you have established the level of analysis and specific project goals, it is necessary to clarify the broader context for adult learners.

CLARIFY THE BROADER CONTEXT FOR ADULT LEARNERS

No program, department, unit, campus, or institution is an island unto itself. Instead, each operates in, is affected by, and contributes to the broader environment in which it exists.

Based on the level of analysis that has been determined, it will be necessary to clarify the broader context for adult learners. How adult-centric are other departments, units, and campus: *highly adult-centric*, where adults are the main constituency and a strategic priority? *Moderately adult-centric*, where adult learners commingle with traditionally aged learners? Or *minimally adult-centric*, where adult learners are a small or emerging constituency and may not represent a strategic priority for the institution?

This clarification of the broader context is important because it speaks to the culture of the campus environment, and can signal whether the broader environment was an early adopter and innovator in adult learning, or whether the campus has been less focused on adult learners. It also signals to you which resources or allies you can marshal for your own analysis and improvement efforts; conversely, it may highlight a culture that might be resistant to adult learner issues. In either event, this clarification can help you focus on the types of leaders and other individuals necessary to secure sponsorship for your efforts.

SECURE APPROPRIATE SPONSORSHIP

The tone at the top can facilitate or impede change efforts in many institutions. Thus, it is necessary to acquire support, endorsement, and sponsorship from key leaders for your efforts to analyze and improve the environment for adult learners. Key diagnostic questions to consider in securing such support include:

- Which key leaders can provide sponsorship for the initiative?
- What is my present relationship to these individuals?
- In what ways can they champion adult learners?
- How have they manifested support for or resistance to adult learner initiatives in the past?
- To what extent can they influence others, shape policies, secure and allocate resources, and make meaningful, sustainable decisions?
- What, specifically, will I need from them to assist me with this initiative?

Securing sponsorship from key leaders and influencers needs to involve more than mere lip service from them. They should be able to articulate the reasons why adult learner issues are important, negotiate for resources to support your efforts, carry your message to other institutional stakeholders on your behalf, and provide advice and guidance in making decisions. They can also be a key ally in changing the culture or implementing specific courses of actions. Leadership sponsors alone, however, will not be sufficient to analyze, improve, and sustain the environment for adult learners. To adequately do so, it is wise to involve other individuals in the effort.

FORM A COMMITTEE OR TASK FORCE

For most individuals in colleges and universities, the thought of serving on yet one more committee or task force may initially elicit groans of resistance. That is why it is critical that leadership support and sponsorship be solicited first, to help signal high-level interest in and the importance of adult learner concerns. From there, carefully selecting individuals who are committed to adult learners will be important in assisting you with your work. In addition to such champions, it will also be necessary to garner sufficient representation from individuals and departments that play a key role in your project's goals. These might include representatives from the registrar and bursar's office, student affairs professionals, faculty governance leaders, academic affairs representatives, the information technology unit, student government leaders, and community and business partners. It is important to let individuals know what you expect them to do on the committee or task force, how often the group will meet, and the specific goals or outcomes you anticipate. Securing commitment and buy-in from their superiors may also be necessary. Finally, you will want to have a facilitator to lead the group, a recorder to capture important notes, and a venue—electronic or otherwise—for storing information collected.

PART II: RESEARCH

Action items in the *Research* phase of the framework include the following:

- Ensure understanding of adult learner issues
- Inventory current practices
- Collect data from additional sources
- Analyze the findings

ENSURE UNDERSTANDING OF ADULT LEARNER ISSUES

After forming the committee or task force, you will need to ensure that its members have a reasonable understanding of adult learner issues, many of which are exemplified by the profiles presented earlier in Chapters Two through Five and in the various readings and resources suggested at the conclusion of each chapter. The group should have an understanding of the broad student, faculty, institutional, and policy issues highlighted in this book; using some of the profiles as a way to introduce or frame the issues might be a worthwhile starting point. At the very least, task force members should understand characteristics of adult learners, their needs and expectations from colleges and universities, and the reasons for and challenges to their participation in higher education. Once you have established background understanding on adult learners, the committee or task force can commence with its work, the first step being an inventory of current practices relating to adult learners.

INVENTORY CURRENT PRACTICES

Based on the level of analysis, context for adult learning, and committee or task force composition, it will be necessary to inventory current practices relating to adult learners within the program, department, unit, or institution, as appropriate. The specific project's goals will obviously inform the exact type of practices to be inventoried, but in general, such practices will typically fall within four broad categories: (1) recruiting and enrolling adult learners; (2) supporting adult learners; (3) engaging and retaining adult learners; and (4) graduating adult learners.

Recruiting and enrolling adult learners includes identifying precisely who are the individual learners in question, including the types of programs likely to be attractive to and needed by adults. It also involves an understanding of prospective students, how and why they apply, and their admissions and subsequent enrollment decisions and patterns. You will also want to identify stakeholders, such as current students, community members, and employers, who can aid in marketing and outreach to adult learners. A listing of recruitment approaches to reaching these adult learners should also be crafted. *Supporting adult learners* speaks to an understanding of the leadership and culture that are present on campus to support adults. It also identifies how services needed by adults are structured, funded, staffed, and used. Given the characteristics and needs of adult learners, it will be necessary to determine the extent to which support and services for adult learners exist on campus. *Engaging and retaining adult students* should identify the faculty behaviors and actions, specific courses, and other experiences and approaches that are valued and needed by adult learners. Finally, *graduating adult learners* should focus on identifying and removing institutional barriers and bottlenecks to persistence, and on facilitating efficient and effective pathways to graduation. This also includes the ongoing relationship management activities that the program or institution has with adult learners after they graduate from or depart the campus.

Open discussion and brainstorming of how committee or task force members perceive the environment is often a good starting point. This anecdotal information alone is not sufficient; thus, the facilitator should insist that inventoried practices rely on objective, evidence-based information, not just on individual perceptions, opinions, memories, feelings, or agendas. After completing an initial and thorough inventory of current practices related to the project's goals, it will be necessary to augment this information with data collected from additional sources.

COLLECT DATA FROM ADDITIONAL SOURCES

Augmenting the inventoried practices with data from additional sources can help to reach more sound conclusions and to develop interventions that embody the experiences, best practices, pitfalls to avoid, and lessons learned from others. This requires both identifying appropriate data sources and collecting relevant information from those sources.

Data collection sources might include relevant stakeholders (such as current, past, or prospective students; faculty; staff; boards of advisors; community or employer representatives), other on-campus programs, departments or units; institutionally collected data; information from the literature (higher education, adult education, and discipline-specific); and information from other colleges or universities. When determining which institutions to benchmark against or from whom to collect data, it is wise to distinguish between peer institutions and aspiration institutions. *Peer institutions* are those colleges and universities that typically have a mission, student body, and programmatic portfolio very similar to your own institution. Because of these similarities, they can provide a useful external context-setting framework by serving as a realistic "comparison other." *Aspiration institutions*, meanwhile, may be quite different from your college or university in terms of mission, student body, and programs, but may nevertheless have a particular adult learning practice that is worthy of consideration or replication. These aspiration institutions are quite often known by their excellent reputations for a particular feature or innovative approach, and this reputation is in many instances recognized by external peers through awards received by the institution and the documentation of the feature or innovative approach through dissemination in the literature.

Collecting relevant information requires several research-oriented methods that will likely already be familiar to committee or task force members. These include interviews, surveys, focus groups, direct observations, competitive intelligence gathering techniques (for example, mystery shopping), and content analysis. In all instances, data collection efforts should strive for validity, relevancy, and objectivity. After identifying data sources and collecting information, it will be necessary to analyze and make meaning from the findings.

ANALYZE THE FINDINGS

In this step, committee or task force members are charged with examining the inventoried practices of their local environment, summarizing the findings from external data collection sources and methods, and determining where there is convergence and, perhaps more important, divergence in the findings. Often referred to as a "gap analysis," this involves determining those practices for which the program, department, unit, or institution is misaligned, as compared with the frequently reported or best practices of others. It is in the analysis of findings that having multiple people and perspectives from the committee or task force is most helpful. The ability to have widespread agreement on where "gaps" exist is helpful in establishing the credibility needed for the next step: an honest appraisal of strengths, weaknesses, opportunities, and threats through a situational analysis.

Part III: Plan

Action items in the *Plan* phase of the framework include the following:

- Conduct a situational analysis
- Identify and prioritize specific actions
- Outline appropriate measures or performance indicators
- Develop an implementation plan
- Communicate with and involve relevant stakeholders
- Provide training, development, and other resources

Conduct a Situational Analysis

A hallmark of strategic planning, the situational analysis can also be used in this case as it relates to adult learning initiatives. The outcomes of the analysis of findings, informed by both internal and external *sources*, can provide a candid portrait of the internal and external *forces* confronting a particular program, department, unit, or institution. Committee or task force members should analyze the findings and broadly categorize them into internal strengths and weaknesses and external opportunities and threats. A facilitated group process, where a candid, excuse-free dialogue and realistic assessment of the present situation—using the evidence-based findings as a guide—is often the best way to garner clear understanding and agreement on what is truly working well and what might need to be addressed or changed. The outcomes of the situational analysis should necessarily lead to the identification and prioritization of specific courses of action.

IDENTIFY AND PRIORITIZE SPECIFIC ACTIONS

From the situational analysis, specific actions can be identified and prioritized. The first task here is to determine the strengths to leverage, weaknesses to correct, opportunities to pursue, and threats to address. Though there will likely be several items in each category, it will be impractical to tackle all of them at once. To aid in the prioritization effort, committee or task force members should review the project's goals, institutional mission and strategic directions, and the broader context for adult learners. What are the specific actions that can be taken that most closely align with each of these?

It is often tempting to tackle the relatively easy, low-hanging fruit, while ignoring or placing the more difficult or ambitious items on the back burner. Thus, it might be helpful to assign a time and resource value to each proposed action. The *time continuum* would have intervals of immediate, short-range, and long-range actions, whereas the *resource* continuum would have intervals of possible actions that are no or low cost, moderate cost, and high cost. The culture, planning cycles, fiscal realities, and needs of each college or university will obviously determine the true definition of concepts such as "immediate," "moderate cost," and so on, as each of these are highly contextual. After the time and resource determinations have been made, and in consultation with appropriate leaders and other stakeholders, specific priorities should be identified and established for each item. From there, appropriate measures or performance indicators and an implementation plan can be established.

OUTLINE APPROPRIATE MEASURES OR PERFORMANCE INDICATORS

As noted in Chapter One, most institutions operate in an environment frequently characterized by accountability and scrutiny from individuals both within and outside of the institution. This dynamic has required a more intentional, explicit, and often transparent allocation of resources, determination of priorities, and development of plans. Thus, before launching into implementation of a specific course of action, it is necessary to begin by outlining how the results of the initiative will ultimately be evaluated and judged for their relative effectiveness in accomplishing a specific aim or purpose. Establishing measures or performance indicators may even be an institutional or external requirement in proposing new programs or initiatives on a large scale, or for determining which investment of significant resources is required. Most measures should typically strive to be relevant to the outcome or objective desired, and should rely on a mix of direct, indirect, quantitative, and qualitative indicators. Whenever possible, these should also be tied to measures already in place within the institution. Once the measures or performance indicators have been outlined, the specific implementation plan can be developed.

DEVELOP AN IMPLEMENTATION PLAN

Based on the items identified and subsequently prioritized from the situational analysis, a specific implementation plan can be developed. Variables such as personnel; the planning and budgeting cycles within the department, unit, or institution; competing and complementary initiatives; and the broader context for adult learning can all have an impact on the ability to implement specific courses of action. Thus, care and attention should be afforded in leveraging the leadership sponsors' knowledge, input, and support to ensure that the implementation plan takes into consideration these many dynamic variables.

Good implementation plans have several components. Typically, a table or chart listing specific objectives is created. Each objective is linked with a time line for implementation, along with the individuals or departments who have specific responsibilities for the objective at certain junctures or milestones along the way. Needed resources, which include physical, financial, human, technological, among others, are identified and the means to secure them are made. Where warranted, a communication and training plan is also detailed. Finally, the sources of data and methods to evaluate or measure effectiveness are typically noted. Many project management software solutions, commercially available or locally developed, can aid in capturing the many moving parts of implementation plan development—something that becomes ever more crucial for large-scale change efforts. The implementation plan can be a useful tool in guiding activities; it can also help to encapsulate, summarize, and communicate with relevant stakeholders the essence of the initiative.

COMMUNICATE WITH AND INVOLVE RELEVANT STAKEHOLDERS

A common axiom in the change management parlance is that individuals are more likely to support something if they have had a hand in its creation. The fact that you are analyzing and improving adult learning environments through such an intentional, representative, and evidence-based process should go a long way toward earning buy-in to your efforts. There still exists, however, a need to communicate with and involve relevant stakeholders in the initiative prior to its implementation. Some of this will likely have occurred through committee or task force representation, leadership sponsorship, data collection methods, and other related activities. Should the initiative be large scale, with potentially widespread impact, such communication and involvement is of utmost importance to ensure ongoing support.

There are several approaches to communicate with and involve others. One is to have the leadership sponsors advocate for the initiative through their existing network of relationships and responsibilities. Another way is to reach out to the individuals or departments likely to be affected and discuss with them the potential impacts such an initiative may have on their scope of work. Yet another way is to hold open "town hall" meetings where concerns or issues can be identified, discussed, or clarified. Finally, using social media technologies and traditional communication channels within the college or university can help ensure that the broader campus community is at least made aware of the forthcoming initiative. Closely related to communicating with and involving others in what you plan to implement is the need to provide training, development, or other resources, as appropriate.

Provide Training, Development, and Other Resources

Implementing some action items may result in a business-as-usual approach to work, because the initiative is similar to already existing activities, and may require using already developed knowledge, skills, competencies, and resources. For some newer action items, implementation must be preceded by the provision of appropriate training and development and the allocation of necessary resources, in order for implementation efforts to succeed. Often, training, development, and resource allocation issues will have been thoughtfully considered in the development of the implementation plan. Such needs may be uncovered during the communication and involvement step described immediately above. In any event, it is necessary to ensure that faculty, staff, and other stakeholders who need to have learning and support receive them prior to the implementation of the initiative. Depending on the complexity associated with a particular action item, there may be a need to pilot-test the intervention before scaling it to its intended target audience or population.

Part IV: Implement

Action items in the *Implement* phase of the framework include the following:

- Pilot-test the intervention
- Implement the intervention
- Evaluate the implementation efforts
- Disseminate the lessons learned

Pilot-Test the Intervention

A pilot test permits a new idea to be tested before widespread rollout or adoption. For innovative, risky, or potentially complex activities, and to get early feedback and make presumably quick alterations, a pilot test may even be most desirable. Considering what, when, how, and with whom to pilot-test an initiative will, again, be highly situational and based on the broader context for adult learning at the institution. In settings where adult learning innovations are well under way, and where the campus culture promotes flexibility and reasonable risk taking, pilot tests may not be needed or practical. However, programs that are early adopters of initiatives such as a new scheduling approach, learning technology, teaching style, or external partnership may want to pilot-test the initiative before investing additional time and resources. Such a pilot test might involve a particular student group, section, or class, semester, faculty member, location, department, or program. Inherent in conducting a pilot test is the willingness and ability to incorporate feedback and lessons learned into enhancing or improving the intervention prior to full-scale implementation.

IMPLEMENT THE INTERVENTION

After all of the hard work of securing buy-in, collecting and analyzing data, making judicious decisions about priorities, and planning for a successful launch, it is now time to implement the intervention. At this stage, the hard work and the outcomes of individual and collective labor should be evident in seeing the action items come to fruition. Even with all the careful analysis and planning, there will inevitably be issues that unintentionally crop up when an intervention is initially implemented. Being open to feedback, responsive to questions, and willing to be flexible and adaptable to the needs of stakeholders can be useful coping mechanisms and management practices in ensuring that the initiative has a reasonably successful beginning. Implementation is a natural time to celebrate and reflect on what was accomplished; however, this step does not signal the end of the journey. Staying the course, evaluating the effort, disseminating lessons learned, and making adult learner issues an ongoing priority are also continual, required steps.

EVALUATE THE IMPLEMENTATION EFFORTS

After an intervention has been implemented, it is necessary to determine the outcomes and impacts of the activities. Because you have already identified and planned for relevant measures or performance indicators, some of the evaluation components will probably be quite evident. Most evaluation professionals use formative and summative approaches to determining effectiveness about a particular program or activity. Formative evaluation collects data and makes judgments early and often, in order to correct for items unaccounted in the planning stages. Summative evaluation takes stock at the natural conclusion of an initiative, or, at the very least, during some agreed-on future ending point in time (for example, the end of the semester or fiscal or academic year).

Evaluation data can help us and others make judgments about our work. Most salient, it can help us make needed changes and ongoing enhancements or improvements to the initiative. In college and university settings, it is also important to link evaluation data back to the mission and strategic directions or priorities of the institution; to coordinate and align with the collecting and reporting of other similar evaluation data; to use evaluation outcomes in building the case for securing additional investments or resources for programs, departments, units, or initiatives; and in disseminating to others the outcomes and lessons learned from your own experiences.

DISSEMINATE THE LESSONS LEARNED

In order for others to benefit from your experiences, perspectives, and outcomes, it is useful to disseminate the lessons learned concerning your efforts at analyzing and improving the environment for adult learners. This is important for several reasons. First, colleagues at your institution and elsewhere can benefit from hearing about the process, strategies, resources, experiences, and outcomes of your work, so that they may replicate certain features that make sense in their own setting. Second, evidence from your work might be profoundly useful in helping other colleagues make their own case for adult learning-centric initiatives. Third, by disseminating your work to external audiences, in particular, you help build on the scholarly base of adult and higher education knowledge, while also helping to legitimize your own work through peer-reviewed processes. Finally, dissemination inevitably leads to the generation of additional ideas for you to consider as you craft policies, practices, and future research agendas.

That, in turn, can embolden you to become a stronger advocate and to help make adult learner issues an ongoing priority in your own college or university environment and elsewhere throughout higher education.

CONCLUSION

At the outset of this book, we identified the changing demographics and composition of the student body in many colleges and universities in the United States. We also presented information on what we know about adult learners, their characteristics, reasons for participation, and the ways institutions have responded to them. In Chapters Two through Six, we engaged you in considering the student, faculty, institutional, and policy issues surrounding adult learners in higher education. Finally, through this experiential approach to analyzing and improving college and university environments for adult learners, in this chapter we have provided a process that can be flexibly used in a variety of settings and levels within institutions. We conclude this volume with a call to you to make adult learner issues an ongoing priority in your own environment. This can be accomplished in ways large and small, and can occur whether you are a faculty or staff member championing for the adult learner at an individual level; a department chair, dean, director, faculty governance leader, or an administrator making decisions that affect programs and resources; or a senior leader, policymaker, or external stakeholder helping to set policy, craft strategy, or influence institutional behaviors and directions. In whatever capacity, level, or context you work, we challenge and encourage you to be a continual voice and advocate for the adult learner in colleges and universities.

REFERENCES

Achacoso, M. V., and Svinicki, M. D. (Eds.). Alternative strategies for evaluating student learning. *New Directions for Teaching and Learning, 100.* San Francisco: Jossey-Bass, 2004.

Alexander, F. K., and Ehrenberg, R. G. (Eds.). Maximizing resources: Universities, public policy, and revenue production *New Directions for Institutional Research, 119.* San Francisco: Jossey-Bass, 2003.

Alfred, M. V. (Ed.). Learning and sociocultural contexts: Implications for adults, community, and workplace education. *New Directions for Adult and Continuing Education, 96.* San Francisco: Jossey-Bass, 2003.

Amey, M. J. (Ed.). Across educational sectors. *New Directions for Community Colleges, 139.* San Francisco: Jossey-Bass, 2007.

Anctil, E. J. Selling higher education: Marketing and advertising America's colleges and universities. *ASHE Higher Education Report, 34*(2). San Francisco: Jossey-Bass, 2008.

Aslanian, C. B. *Adult students today.* New York: The College Board, 2001.

Astin, A. W. *What matters in college? Four critical years revisited.* San Francisco: Jossey-Bass, 1997.

Astin, A. W., Keup, J. R., and Lindholm, J. A. A decade of changes in undergraduate education: A national study of system "transformation." *Review of Higher Education, 25*(2), 141–162, 2002.

Barkley, E. F., Cross, K. P., and Major, C. H. *Collaborative learning techniques: A handbook for college faculty.* San Francisco: Jossey-Bass, 2004.

Bash, L. *Adult learners in the academy.* Bolton, MA: Anker, 2003.

Bash, L. (Ed.). *Best practices in adult learning.* Bolton, MA: Anker, 2005.

Blakely, P. N., and Tomlin, A. H. (Eds.). *Adult education: Issues and developments.* New York: NOVA, 2008.

Bradley, J. S., and Graham, S. W. The effect of educational ethos and campus involvement on self-reported college outcomes for traditional and nontraditional undergraduates. *Journal of College Student Development, 41*(5), 488–502, 2000.

Braxton, J. M. (Ed.). The role of the classroom in college student persistence. *New Directions for Teaching and Learning, 115.* San Francisco: Jossey-Bass, 2008.

Braxton, J. M., Hirschy, A. S., and McClendon, S. A. Understanding and reducing college student departure. *ASHE-ERIC Higher Education Report, 30*(3). San Francisco: Jossey-Bass, 2004.

Brookfield, S. D., and Preskill, S. *Discussion as a way of teaching: Tools and techniques for democratic classrooms* (2nd ed.). San Francisco: Jossey-Bass, 2005.

Bruffee, K. A. *Collaborative learning: Higher education, interdependence, and the authority of knowledge.* Baltimore: Johns Hopkins University Press, 1993.

Bueschel, A. C., and Venezia, A. (Eds.). Policies and practices to improve student preparation and success. *New Directions for Community Colleges, 145.* San Francisco: Jossey-Bass, 2009.

Burge, E. J. (Ed.). The strategic use of learning technologies. *New Directions for Adult and Continuing Education, 88.* San Francisco: Jossey-Bass, 2001.

Burke, J. C. (Ed.). *Achieving accountability in higher education: Balancing public, academic, and market demands.* San Francisco: Jossey-Bass, 2004.

Caffarella, R. S. *Planning programs for adult learners: A practical guide for educators, trainers, and staff developers.* San Francisco: Jossey-Bass, 2001.

Cervero, R. M., Wilson, A. L., and Associates. *Adult education and the struggle for knowledge and power in society.* San Francisco: Jossey-Bass, 2001.

Chickering, A. W., and Gamson, Z. F. Seven principles for good practice in undergraduate education. *AAHE Bulletin, 39*(7), 3–7. Washington, DC: American Association for Higher Education, 1987.

Chickering, A. W., and Gamson, Z. F. (Eds.). Applying the seven principles of good practice in undergraduate education. *New Directions for Teaching and Learning, 47.* San Francisco: Jossey-Bass, 1991.

Clark, M. C., and Caffarella, R. S. (Eds.). An update on adult development theory: New ways of thinking about the life course. *New Directions for Adult and Continuing Education, 84.* San Francisco: Jossey-Bass, 2000.

Coomes, M. D., and DeBard, R. (Eds.). Serving the millennial generation: *New Directions for Student Services, 106.* San Francisco: Jossey-Bass, 2004.

Crady, T., and Sumner, J. (Eds.). Key issues in new student enrollment. *New Directions for Student Services, 118.* San Francisco: Jossey-Bass, 2007.

Cranton, P. *Understanding and promoting transformative learning: A guide for educators of adults.* San Francisco: Jossey-Bass, 2006.

Dickeson, R. C. *Prioritizing academic programs and services: Reallocating resources to achieve strategic balance.* San Francisco: Jossey-Bass, 1999.

Dotolo, L. G., and Noftsinger, J. B., Jr. (Eds.). Leveraging resources through partnerships. *New Directions for Higher Education, 120*. San Francisco: Jossey-Bass, 2002.

Erickson, B. L., Peters, C. B., and Strommer, D. W. *Teaching first-year college students*. San Francisco: Jossey-Bass, 2006.

Finger, M., and Asun, J. M. *Adult education at the crossroads: Learning our way out*. New York: Zed Books, 2001.

Fink, L. D. *Creating significant learning experiences: An integrated approach to designing college courses*. San Francisco: Jossey-Bass, 2003.

Flint, T. A., Zakos, P., and Frey, R. *Best practices in adult learning: A self-evaluation workbook for colleges and universities*. Dubuque, IA: Kendall/Hunt, 2002.

Hadfield, J. Recruiting and retaining adult students. *New Directions for Students Services, 102*. San Francisco: Jossey-Bass, 2003.

Hansman, C. A., and Sissel, P. A. (Eds.). Understanding and negotiating the political landscape of adult education. *New Directions for Adult and Continuing Education, 91*. San Francisco: Jossey-Bass, 2001.

Houle, C. O. *The design of education* (2nd ed.). San Francisco: Jossey-Bass, 1996.

Johnstone, S. M., Ewell, P., and Paulson, K. *Student learning as academic currency*. Washington, DC: American Council on Education, 2002.

Junco, R., and Timm, D. M. (Eds.). Using emerging technologies to enhance student engagement. *New Directions for Student Services, 124*. San Francisco: Jossey-Bass, 2009.

Kasworm, C. E. Adult meaning making in the undergraduate classroom. *Adult Education Quarterly, 53*(2), 81–97, 2003a.

Kasworm, C. E. From the adult student's perspective: Accelerated degree programs. *New Directions for Adult and Continuing Education, 97*, 17–27, 2003b.

Kasworm, C. E. Setting the stage: Adults in higher education. *New Directions for Student Services, 102*, 3–10, 2003c.

Keeton, M., Sheckley, B., and Griggs, J. *Effectiveness and efficiency in higher education for adults: A guide for fostering learning*. Dubuque, IA: Kendall/Hunt, 2002.

Kell, P., Shore, S., and Singh, M. *Adult education @ 21st century*. New York: Peter Lang, 2004.

Kilgore, D., and Rice, P. J. (Eds.). Meeting the special needs of adult students. *New Directions for Student Services, 102*. San Francisco: Jossey-Bass, 2003.

Kim, K., Hagedorn, M., Williamson, J., and Chapman, C. *Participation in adult education and lifelong learning 2000–01*. Retrieved February 2,

2010, from www.nces.ed.gov/pubs2004/2004050.pdf. Washington, DC: U.S. Department of Education, 2004.

King, J. E., Anderson, E. L., and Corrigan, M. E. (Eds.). Changing student attendance patterns: Challenges for policy and practice. *New Directions for Higher Education, 121.* San Francisco: Jossey-Bass, 2003.

Kinser, K. From main street to wall street: For-profit higher education. *ASHE Higher Education Report, 31*(5). San Francisco: Jossey-Bass, 2006.

Knowles, M. S. *The modern practice of adult education: From pedagogy to andragogy* (2nd ed.). Englewood Cliffs, NJ: Prentice Hall/Cambridge, 1980.

Kramer, G. L. (Ed.). *Faculty advising examined: Enhancing the potential of college faculty as advisors.* San Francisco: Jossey-Bass, 2003.

Kuh, G. D. *High-impact educational practices: What they are, who has access to them, and why they matter.* Washington, DC: Association of American Colleges and Universities, 2008.

Kuh, G. D., Kinzie, J., Buckley, J., Bridges, B., and Hayek, J. Piecing together the student success puzzle: Research, propositions, and recommendations. *ASHE Higher Education Report, 32*(5). San Francisco: Jossey-Bass, 2007.

Kuh, G. D., Kinzie, J., Schuh, J. H., Whitt, E. J., and Associates. *Student success in college: Creating conditions that matter.* San Francisco: Jossey-Bass, 2005.

Laanan, F. S. (Ed.). Understanding students in transition: Trends and issues. *New Directions for Student Services, 114.* San Francisco: Jossey-Bass, 2006.

Lapovsky, L., and Klinger, D. (Eds.). Strategic financial challenges for higher education: How to achieve quality, accountability, and innovation. *New Directions for Higher Education, 140.* San Francisco: Jossey-Bass, 2008.

Lazerson, M., Wagener, U., and Shumanis, N. What makes a revolution? Teaching and learning in higher education, 1980–2000. *Change, 32*(3), 2000.

Levine, A. The remaking of the American university. *Innovative Higher Education, 25*(4), 2001.

Light, R. J. *Making the most of college: Students speak their minds.* Cambridge, MA: Harvard University Press, 2001.

Maehl, W. H. *Lifelong learning at its best: Innovative practices in adult credit programs.* San Francisco: Jossey-Bass, 1999.

Martyn, M. The hybrid online model: Good practice. *Educause Quarterly, 26*(1), 18–23, 2003.

Massey, W. F. *Honoring the trust: Quality and cost containment in higher education.* Bolton, MA: Anker, 2003.

Matkin, G. W. Adult degree programs: How money talks, and what it tells. *New Directions for Adult and Continuing Education, 103,* 61–71, 2004.

Merriam, S. B., and Brockett, R. G. *The profession and practice of adult education: An introduction.* San Francisco: Jossey-Bass, 2007.

Merriam, S. B., Caffarella, R. S., and Baumgartner, L. M. *Learning in adulthood: A comprehensive guide.* San Francisco: Jossey-Bass, 2006.

Mezirow, J. *Fostering critical reflection in adulthood: A guide to transformative and emancipatory learning.* San Francisco: Jossey-Bass, 1990.

Mezirow, J. *Learning as transformation: Critical perspectives on a theory in progress.* San Francisco: Jossey-Bass, 2000.

Miller, T. E., Bender, B. E., and Schuh, J. H. *Promoting reasonable expectations: Aligning student and institutional views of the college experience.* San Francisco: Jossey-Bass, 2005.

Nesbit, T. (Ed.). Adult education and social class. *New Directions for Adult and Continuing Education, 106.* San Francisco: Jossey-Bass, 2005.

Newman, F., Couturier, L. K., and Sessa, D. The new competitive arena. *Change, 33*(5), 2001.

Pappas, J., and Jerman, J. (Eds.). Developing and delivering adult degree programs. *New Directions for Adult and Continuing Education, 103.* San Francisco: Jossey-Bass, 2004.

Perna, L. W., and Thomas, S. L. Theoretical perspectives on student success: Understanding the contributions of the disciplines. *ASHE Higher Education Report, 34*(1). San Francisco: Jossey-Bass, 2008.

Reed, S. C., and Marienau, C. (Eds.). Linking adults with community: Promoting civic engagement through community based learning. *New Directions for Adult and Continuing Education, 118.* San Francisco: Jossey-Bass, 2008.

Reindl, T. The road ahead: Access and success in American higher education. *College and University, 77*(4), 2002.

Rice, P. J. Adult student service office. *New Directions for Student Services, 102,* 53–57, 2003.

Ross-Gordon, J. M. Adult learners in the classroom. *New Directions for Student Services, 102,* 43–52, 2003.

Schroeder, C. C. Supporting the new students in higher education today. *Change, 35*(2), 2003.

Smith, B. L., MacGregor, J., Matthews, R., and Gabelnick, F. *Learning communities: Reforming undergraduate education.* San Francisco: Jossey-Bass, 2004.

Spangler, M. S. (Ed.). Developing successful partnerships with business and the community. *New Directions for Community Colleges, 119.* San Francisco: Jossey-Bass, 2002.

Swail, W. S. Higher education and the new demographics. *Change, 34*(4), 14–23, 2002.

Tagg, J. *The learning paradigm college.* Bolton, MA: Anker, 2003.

Tennant, M., and Pogson, P. *Learning and change in the adult years: A developmental perspective.* San Francisco: Jossey-Bass, 2002.

Thomas, A. M. Prior learning assessment: The quiet revolution. In A. L. Wilson and E. R. Hayes (Eds.), *Handbook of adult and continuing education* (pp. 508–522). San Francisco: Jossey-Bass, 2000.

Tinto, V. *Leaving college: Rethinking the causes and cures of student attrition* (2nd ed.). Chicago: University of Chicago Press, 1994.

Townsend, B. K., and Dougherty, K. J. (Eds.). Community college missions in the 21st century. *New Directions for Community Colleges, 136.* San Francisco: Jossey-Bass, 2007.

Twigg, C. A. Improving quality and reducing cost: Designs for effective learning. *Change, 35*(4), 22–29, 2003.

U.S. Department of Education, National Center for Education Statistics. *Digest of education statistics.* Washington, DC: Author, 2002.

Vella, J. *Taking learning to task: Creative strategies for teaching adults.* San Francisco: Jossey-Bass, 2000.

Vella, J. *Learning to listen, learning to teach: The power of dialogue in educating adults.* San Francisco: Jossey-Bass, 2002.

Vella, J. *On teaching and learning: Putting the principles and practices of dialogue education into action.* San Francisco: Jossey-Bass, 2007.

Wilson, A. L., and Hayes, E. R. *Handbook of adult and continuing education.* San Francisco: Jossey-Bass, 2009.

Wlodkowski, R. J. *Enhancing adult motivation to learn: A comprehensive guide for teaching all adults* (3rd ed.). San Francisco: Jossey-Bass, 2008.

Wlodkowski, R. J., and Kasworm, C. E. (Eds.). Accelerated learning for adults: The promise and practice of intensive educational formats. *New Directions for Adult and Continuing Education, 97.* San Francisco: Jossey-Bass, 2003.

Wolf, M. A. (Ed.). Adulthood: New terrain. *New Directions for Adult and Continuing Education, 108.* San Francisco: Jossey-Bass, 2006.

Yorks, L., and Kasl, E. (Eds.). Collaborative inquiry as a strategy for adult learning. *New Directions for Adult and Continuing Education, 94.* San Francisco: Jossey-Bass, 2002.

INDEX